What Do I Do with My Major in Psychology

What Do I Do with My Major in Psychology

Kathy Sexton-Radek, Ph.D.
Elmhurst College

Patrice Paul, Ph.D.
Aurora University

iUniverse, Inc.
New York Lincoln Shanghai

What Do I Do with My Major in Psychology

iUniverse, Inc.

For information address:
iUniverse
2021 Pine Lake Road, Suite 100
Lincoln, NE 68512
www.iuniverse.com

ISBN: 0-595-28954-1

Contents

Chapter 1

Living Outside the Box: Life as a Psychology Major

Join Your Psychology Department

Since early childhood, we've been encouraged to join in events. This age-old message conveys an adage to us to help in our social development. The essence of this phrase implies advice for successful commitment as well. By joining the Psychology department, the Psychology major is able to let themselves become known to the professors. In so doing they are able to have an "inside track," so to speak, on what is happening in the department in terms of programming, seminars and talks, and job opportunities. Importantly, we advise the joining of the department to learn more about courses in psychology and research activities of the faculty. In so doing, you will provide yourself with potential opportunities to gain knowledge about the field and participate on research projects. Think of this as an investment in an exploration of what the psychology major is about.

By 2005 it is estimated that 73,000 students will graduate with a major in psychology. "What Do I Do with My Major in Psychology?" was designed to help the psychology major formulate and plan their ideas about their study of psychology.

This investment in an exploration of what the psychology major is about will provide the undergraduate with important, useful resource information.

- A college degree is still a good investment.
- Job seekers are ad.vised to research the job market, sharpen their communication skills, and get experience while still in college.
- The fastest growing occupations are predicted to be in health, engineering, and computer science.

Strengths from interpersonal skills, written and oral communication and analytical thinking are developed with a major in psychology. This is attractive to employers and places a psychology major in an employable position. Employers want students who understand human behavior.

Vision and Mission of the Psychology Major

In a liberal arts college the focus of the major is within the context of a liberal arts education. Historically, liberal arts education meant "liberation from ignorance." A core set of areas of knowledge from which privileged individuals studied became known as liberal arts education. In this tradition, students in a liberal arts college environment study courses from a framework of courses in addition to their major area of study. The outcome of liberal arts education is considered to produce an educated person. The college dedicates itself to the development of humane values, the skills of critical and creative inquiry, the capacity and desire to serve others, commitment to meaningful work, understanding of global interdependence, and responsible citizenship.

In this setting, a psychology major is oftentimes defined by how it will prepare students to study psychological theory and methods. Some colleges broaden this to include the application and interpretation of psychological science to everyday life.

While university settings for a psychology major do not differ in their mission to prepare students, compared to liberal arts colleges, they do not place the conceptual linkage to an overarching goal. The psychology major functions as a small company necessary to the larger economy that has interdependence and maintains independence.

Important to this presentation is that the student should be aware of the specific goals of the psychology major at their college or university. In learning these goals, the student will be able to develop a clear sense of what is expected course by course and at the completion of the major. This accumulation of expectancies in a course by course manner and overall will help the student to develop perspectives and eventually synthesize the psychological material they learn.

Is Psychology the Major for You?

One way to access this information is to discuss the direction of the psychology major with a faculty member at your school. A well planned sequence of how the progress of a psychology class should match up to goals for the major. An investigation of what psychological knowledge should be learned and in what manner would be fruitful.

A good resource for job outlook information can be found on the American Psychological Association web page (www.apa.org). In addition to this, APA surveys undergraduate departments about employment—Bureau of Educational Affairs office of APA. In a recent publication of the APA <u>Monitor</u>, it was stated that new doctorates begin their careers in hospital settings and managed care before branching off into independent practice.

Most undergraduates join the work force after graduation with 40% of psychology majors from four-year schools choosing immediate full time employment. The most common job offer is in the sales area followed by management trainee. Landrum (2001) reported "ten top skills" that employers look for in psychology majors. Problem-solving skills and ability to work on teams were two of the skills and "people" interest for business jobs. Lloyd (2001) explained that getting involved in extra-curricular activities is critical to your success in the future. So, the jobs are available in psychology!

Core learning goals have been identified by the APA Board of Educational Affairs for the undergraduate major in psychology.

1. Theory and Content of Psychology
2. Research Methods in Psychology
3. Critical Thinking Skills in Psychology
4. Application of Psychology
5. Values in Psychology
6. Information and Technological Literacy
7. Communication Skills
8. Sociocultural and Intellectual Awareness
9. Personal Development
10 Career Planning and Development

These aspiring achievement goals represent a guideline for the design and outcome of a Psychology major. How does your department measure up?

Hogan (1991) proposed the selection of courses in Psychology that are related to career issues and skills. Perlman and McCann (1999) noted that current curriculums in Psychology are largely in terms of experimental/developmental, biological, clinical and social/developmental courses rather than vocational/career type. Some departments offer overview courses that provide the beginning student with valuable information about the major (Dillinger & Landrum, 2002; Landrum, 2001; Morgan & Karschgens, 2001).

It is also helpful to consult career books specific to the field, How to Manage Your Career in Psychology provides an overview of daily roles and responsibilities. The publication of the American Psychological Association offers articles on this topic on a regular basis (Murray, 2002). The internet has a myriad of resources as you might have imagined (Murray, 2002).

Major Entry #1

Do a brief review of your objectives and skills as they relate to your choice of the psychology major. Here we go:

What do you want to study in psychology?

What are your writing and research experiences?

If you are just starting out, how can you get these?

If you have observed a psychologist working or have looked up what a psychologist does—what interests you the most?

If you have not talked to a psychologist, set up an informational interview to see how his/her career builds on the core areas listed on page 4.

Take one of the core areas listed on page 4 and describe what you know and would like to know about that area.

Chapter 2

The Academic Classroom

INSTANT MESSAGE: YOU, YOUR PSYCHOLO-GY MAJOR, YOUR CAREER
GETTING THE MOST FROM YOUR UNDER-GRADUATE YEARS

Many students are interested in applying for graduate school immediately following completion of their undergraduate education. Other students want to take time off after graduation to work or gain other types of experiences. And others choose to work in the field of psychology in entry-level positions. Regardless of when you are thinking of applying to graduate school, there are ways to best maximize your time as an undergraduate. What follows is a general timeline for various accomplishments to enhance your future prospects.

FRESHMEN YEAR: ORIENTATION

This is your time to explore your institution. Get to know the academic programs, academic departments, academic expectations, and academic resources. Read your catalog and discuss the importance and relevance of the catalog with your advisor, and become familiar with your institution's policies (e.g., academic dishonesty, conduct, graduation requirements). Become familiar with the general education requirements as well as those for your intended major. Learn how to navigate registration (e.g., add/drop and special forms). Develop your time management skills and study habits/skills. Begin exploration of your major, interests, and career possibilities while conceptualizing your academic plan. Use this time to get to know the faculty in the psychology department. Each faculty member has unique research and practice interests. Begin to cultivate a relationship with those who have interests similar to yours.

COLLEGE CLASSROOM EXPECTATIONS

- You can expect that the level of challenges in courses at the college/university level will be more difficult than high school courses.
- You should spend at least triple the time in class studying and working on class assignments.
- In your courses, instructors will expect you to actively participate, contact them if you are having problems, and be responsible for material covered in class.
- Academically, one of the biggest challenges of your first year will be managing your time.
- The first step to success is to attend class.
- Your syllabus is a guide to your course and a valuable source of information (e.g., materials covered, due dates for assignments, dates of exams). Always consult your syllabus first before asking your instructor about such issues. Often the answer will be found in the syllabus.
- Always contact your instructor about a class absence as soon as possible.
- If you arrive late, quietly take a convenient seat.
- Put cell phones, pagers, electronic organizers to vibrate or turn them off.

SOPHOMORE YEAR

This is the time to start solidifying your career and academic goals through more in-depth reflection with your faculty mentors and advisor. Consider participating in shadowing opportunities or communicate with program alumni to further explore your interest. Begin to take courses that build a tract in a specialty area of psychology that interests you. Should service learning opportunities be available in your courses, consider participating. Join academic clubs and participate to your fullest extent.

JUNIOR YEAR

Preparing yourself for entrance into graduate school in psychology is a very involved process. It can be overwhelming if you look at the big picture. You are best advised to focus on the details, which begin to rear their head during your junior year. This is the time when you want to start building your resume into your curriculum vitae. Aside from focusing your coursework toward your goals, you will want to find involvement in other activities. Consider participating in an internship or fieldwork program should one be available at your institution. If not, consider volunteering with the mentorship of a faculty member. Get involved in research and go the extra mile to secure authorship on any presentations/publications that might result. (The importance of practical experience and research experience are detailed in a separate chapter in this book.) You will also want to start preparing to take the GRE.

Importantly, contact graduate programs you are interested in attending and ask to receive their course catalog and application packet. This will give you a chance to review what programs require of their applicants. You will also be able to make effective comparisons between the course offerings at various institutions. This is also a good time to start researching the faculty research interests at graduate schools by looking them up in PsychInfo. The more research you can do on an institution, the better you can determine their fit to your goals.

SENIOR YEAR

During your senior year, you will want to take your GREs and finalize your graduate school selection. You will want to collect your letters of recommendation. These letters should reflect your academic skills, personal strengths, practical experience, and potential in the field of psychology. It is to your advantage to obtain letters from a diverse group of people who have had intimate experience with you (e.g., faculty mentor, classroom instructor, research supervisor, field supervisor). Do not be afraid to ask faculty for help with writing your personal/professional statement and prepare a C.V. Always be mindful of the application deadlines for graduate school. Your application must be complete for it to be considered for review.

ONE LAST THOUGHT

Throughout your four years, you also need to keep an eye on your grade point average (GPA). Most everyone has a grade in a course or two that do not necessarily reflect your true abilities. Remember that your graduate school application packet, not just one component, represents you. Be sure to maximize your undergraduate experience in order to produce a packet that is reflective of your abilities, achievements, and potential.

Now let's keep to the matter at hand, your classes and your decision to major in psychology. It will be to your benefit to check you academic skills. What follows are some suggestions designed to enhance your college experience—academically. The checklist on page 11 can be used as a beginning guide to selecting your psychology courses we well as identifying a well-matched minor.

Major Entry #2

Answer the following questions:

What are my academic interests? What kinds of topics do I like? List them.

Where are my strengths academically.

I perform well in _____
because

I perform well in _____
because

I perform well in _____
because

SOME LEARNING STRATEGIES

After completing Major Entry #2 you will have some idea of your academic strengths. Review the following sections to learn about strategies of learning.

TIME MANAGEMENT

- create a realistic schedule
- plan two hours of study for each one hour of class
- set deadlines and plan your weeks ahead of time
- use "waiting" time effectively (e.g., review notes between classes)
- allow for flexibility—unexpected events cannot always be avoided
- schedule "me" time—time for fun
- watch the work schedule—remember, school is your primary job
- prioritize important things to do
- analyze how, when, and where you spend your time
- do not always say "yes" to social activities.

STUDY SKILLS

- begin studying for exams on the **first day** of class
- review class notes as soon after class as you can
- at least once a week (daily for some classes), review notes back to the beginning of the term
- take a 10 minute break for every hour of studying
- attend Study Skills Workshops in the Learning Center

TEST TAKING

REVIEW*

- daily before and after class
- weekly—reread book and lecture notes
- make practice test questions

TOOLS*

- create your own study list of major points
- create lists and sequences your mind can understand
- develop flashcards of test items, such as terms, practice, questions, and formulas

TESTS*

- know the format (essay, multiple choice, T/F)
- read all instructions carefully
- proofread once you have finished.

ACTIVE VS. PASSIVE LEARNING

Adopt the attitude that your college teachers are responsible for no more than presenting ideas and information to you. Assume that it is your responsibility to learn. Students are often conditioned by magazines, television, and movies to be *passive* learners. Consequently, they expect to be entertained by their textbooks and instructors. The only instructors or assignments these students pay attention to are those which catch their attention, just as professional entertainers do. However, college teachers are not encouraged to be entertainers; being an entertainer in the classroom is viewed as unprofessional at most schools.

Consider developing the attitude that you are going to become an *active* learner, and that you are going to get the most out of every class. You have paid your money, so get what you paid for. You are the consumer! You can make even the most boring class interesting by assuming that every teacher has useful information for you. Be determined to learn everything that you can from each of your teachers and textbooks. Realize that the best investment that you will every make is in yourself. You may lose your job or your money, but no one can every take your education away from you.

While these results clearly suggest that attending class helps students to increase their performance, there are many other ways in which assuming an active strategy towards your education can enable you to achieve academic success. Consider the following pairs of active vs. passive strategies, and whenever possible, choose the active approach.

Passive ➔ Just sit in lectures because you have to be there.
Active ➔ Come to lectures prepared, pay attention, take notes, and ask questions.

Passive ➔ Buy used books that already have the important points underlined.
Active ➔ Buy new books and do the underlining yourself.

Passive ➔ Borrow and use lecture notes from someone who has already taken the class.
Active ➔ Take your own lecture notes.

Passive ➔ Read assignments just to get them over with.
Active ➔ Skim assignments first, make up a list of questions that you would like to answer, and then read the assignments to answer the questions.
Passive ➔ Pay attention only to the grades you earned on tests when they are returned.
Active ➔ Study returned tests carefully so that you don't make the same mistakes again.

Passive ➔ Don't work any harder than you have to in any class.
Active ➔ Volunteer to help someone in your class who is having a tough time

WHAT DID I JUST READ?
HOW TO READ A TEXTBOOK FOR MAXI-MUM COMPREHENSION

A. Getting to know your textbook
    1. Read the introduction or preface to discover the author's orientation
    2. Read chapter titles to determine the organizational structure
    3. Become familiar with its pedagogical aids
        a. table of contents
        b. chapter outlines
        c. boldface print for new items
        d. end-of-section or end-of-chapter summaries
        e. questions at beginning or end of chapter
        f. appendixes
        g. glossary
        h. recommended reading list
        i. chapter summaries and learning objectives (in this study guide)

B. The SQ4R method
    1. Survey—should take only 5-10 minutes for a 50 page chapter and save percent of study time
        a. chapter title
        b. chapter outline
        c. introduction or first paragraph
        d. section headings
        e. illustrations and their captions
        f. section summaries
        g. questions at the end of the chapter
    2. Question
        a. write questions you would like to answer from assignment on 3x5 cards.
        b. unanswered questions are bothersome, and you will need to answer them.
        c. reading becomes more purposeful if you have questions to answer
        d. cautions:
            1. do not overload yourself with question
            2. do not make your questions too elaborate
            3. be flexible; add, omit, or change your questions if necessary
    3. Read
        a. read until you come to the answer of a question

   b. study the answer and try to understand it in your own words

   c. go to the next step

4. Recite

   a. close the book

   b. repeat the answer back to yourself in your own words

   c. open the book, and compare your answer to the book's answer

   d. if it is not acceptable, go back to the last step and repeat it

   e. if it is acceptable, go to the next step

5. Write

   a. write the answer to the question (and page number) on the reverse side of the card

   b. repeat steps 3-5 until you have written all the answers to your questions

6. Review

   a. use the cards as flash cards

   b. review immediately after finishing the assignment

   c. review at least three more times, once immediately before the test

A Note Of Caution about the SQ4R Method: My experience with the SQ4R method leads me to believe that not all students use all six stages to help them study in a goal-directed and systematic manner. For example, you may find that the judicious use of the "recitation" stages is sufficient for you to increase your understanding and performance. In any event, you should consider using some or all of the components, especially if the results of your exams suggest that your previous study methods are not sufficiently effective. One of the major themes of your textbook is that wide individual differences exist among people in almost all aspects of their behavior and mental processes. Studying and test-taking are no exceptions to this theme. Use this opportunity to perform a "study-technique analysis" on your self that will produce results that can increase your performance not only in this class, but in your other classes as well. The more familiar you are with your mental processes, the more successfully you can use them to your academic advantage.

Monitor your reading to ensure comprehension. As you read an assignment, ask yourself the following questions: "Do I really understand this, or do I need to read it again," "Did I get lost several paragraphs ago," "If so, where do I need to begin my review," "Am I just reciting by rote or do I understand this well enough for the test." Your answers to these questions will help to guide your reading habits to ensure that you are actually learning the material, rather than just allowing your eyes to pass over the words so that you can say that you have finished the assignment when you finish reading the last page.

Remember, textbooks are expensive, and smart students get their money's worth from them. Therefore, become familiar with the pedagogical aids in your books. Their purpose is to help you learn in the most efficient manner possible. Active learning produces better understanding and retention than passive learning. Therefore, give yourself a purpose for reading an assignment (i.e., ask yourself specific questions) and then read the assignment to discover their answers. Do NOT read an assignment just to get it out of the way. An important part of studying is the active identification of the main points of the material you are trying to learn. This process forces you to discriminate between important and less important material as you read, and helps you to review more efficiently. To that end, highlight or underline the important terms, concepts, and relationships in your textbook. (Hint: Use your highlighter or pen sparingly; using them too much indicates an inability to identify genuinely important information and makes reviewing more difficult.)

People learn best when they experience new material in a number of ways (e.g., by seeing it, hearing it, and doing it). Therefore reading, reciting, and writing the answers to your questions will help you learn the information in an assignment more effectively than just reading it. Meaningful and personally relevant information is learned more quickly and retained longer than material perceived to be meaningless or irrelevant. Therefore, before your read an assignment, become familiar with it, understand why you are reading it, and think of ways to relate its contents to your own life experiences (i.e., make it personally relevant).

The best way to prepare for any new task—such as a test—is to prepare for that task under the same conditions in which you will engage in it. Therefore, writing answers to questions you have constructed is an excellent method to prepare for a test. The vast majority of information is forgotten very quickly if it is not practiced. If it is practiced on several occasions, it is much more likely to be remembered. Therefore, it is very important to practice recalling information in your own words as you read it and to review it several times after you have finished reading it.

IT HELPS TO HAVE SOMETHING TO WRITE WITH:
Strategies to Maximize Note-Taking Efficiency

A. Why take notes?
  1. To help you retain material
  2. To sustain your attention in class
  3. To engage you actively in the class
  4. To force you to think about the lecture content
  5. To provide material to review as you prepare for a test
  6. To point out the strengths and weaknesses of your listening skills
B. Techniques to increase note-taking efficiency
  1. Learn how your professors communicate to you that something is important. You may observe the following cues:
    a. repeat it
    b. stop pacing
    c. make eye contact
    d. give examples of it
    e. write it on the board
    f. make dramatic gestures
    g. change their tone of voice
    h. say "in summary" or "in conclusion"
    i. give you time to write it in your notes
    j. follow it with a period of dramatic silence
    k. include it in their introduction to a lecture.
  2. Try hard to understand the organizational structure of lectures
    a. pay close attention during introductions and summaries
    b. use the outline method of note-taking whenever possible
  3. Develop a "speed hand"
    a. use abbreviations
    b. keep a list of your abbreviations and their meanings
  4. Date your notes
    a. this helps to keep them in order if you remove pages from your notebook
    b. dating pages makes it easier for professors to answer your questions if you can tell them the date of the lecture.
C. Six principles of efficient note-taking
  1. Be flexible: adapt your note-taking style to different lecturing styles

2. Once you select a successful style, stay with it
3. Schedule a time as soon after class as possible to review your notes
4. Take no more notes than are necessary for complete understanding
5. Use your "speed hand" whenever possible
6. Your notes should be immediately clear when you re-read them; if they are not, ask a reliable fellow student, the teaching assistant, or your professor for clarification as soon as possible.

You will not attend to, understand, or retain lecture material if you approach lectures in a passive manner. Therefore, do not attend class just so that your professor doesn't count you absent.

Go to class prepared to actively learn the material that will be given in the lecture. People learn best and retain the most when they experience new material in a number of ways (e.g., by seeing it, hearing it, thinking about it, and doing it). Therefore, pay close attention to what your professor does and says during lectures, try your best to understand the organization of the lecture, and take notes that are as simple bust as complete as possible.

The vast majority of information is forgotten very quickly if it is not practiced. If it is practiced on several occasions, it is much less likely to be forgotten. Therefore, it is very important to re-read your notes as soon as possible after a class and to review them several times before a test.

The more familiar you are with a person who is speaking to you, the more able you are to interpret his or her message. Therefore, do your best to pick up the subtle, and sometimes not so subtle, cues that professors give during their lectures that indicate that they are talking about something they consider important enough to be asked on a test.

People understand and retain organized material far better than material that is unorganized. Therefore, work hard to understand the organizational structure of a lecture as you hear it. This will be harder during some lectures than others, but it is extremely important that you do it in all lectures.

The information that your professor presents in lectures is as important as the material from your textbook. Therefore, study your lecture notes as carefully as you study the textbook (e.g. highlight main ideas, make up possible test questions from the, and review them immediately before a test).

HOW TO MAXIMIZE TEST-TAKING PERFORMANCE

A. Objective tests—scores are same for all graders
    1. Types: matching, true-false, multiple-choice, and fill-in-the-blank
    2. Type of material most often tested is factual
    3. Cognitive functions required: recognition and decision making
    4. Preparation strategies
        a. To increase retention of new material
            i. use SQ4r cards as flash cards
            ii. quiz classmates on key terms and concepts
            iii. use mnemonics (i.e., memory strategies)
        b. To increase understanding of new material
            i. make up concrete examples of abstract ideas
            ii. apply new material to your everyday life
        c. To anticipate questions and avoid mistakes
            i. review and learn from previous tests in the class
            ii. try to identify reasons why you missed previous questions.
    5. Test-taking strategies for objective tests
        a. read directions carefully and ask for clarification if necessary
        b. read all questions thoroughly before you answer any of them
        c. answer the easiest questions first and leave the hardest for last
        d. read all the answers to each question before you select one
        e. use the process of elimination to increase your success on hard questions
        f. avoid distracters containing absolutes (e.g., everyone or never)
        g. use remaining time to check answers
        h. answer changing is okay, but know your answer-changing style
        i. if your professor allows you to write on the test paper, cross out wrong answers and underline critical words in the questions to help you focus on j. the right answer
B. Subjective tests—scores can depend upon characteristics of graders
    1. Types: essay or short answer
    2. Types of materials most often tested: conceptual and theoretical
    3. Cognitive functions require: comprehension, application, analysis, synthesis, and evaluation
    4. Preparation strategies
        a. attempt to anticipate questions (2nd step of SQ4R)
        b. practice writing answers to anticipated questions (4th step of SQ4R)
        c. use mnemonics to help you remember main parts of answers

     d. review previous tests in the class to help you identify weaknesses in your pattern of answering subjective test questions

  5. Test-taking strategies for subjective tests

     a. read directions carefully and ask for clarification if necessary

     b. determine how much time to spend on each question

     c. begin with the easiest question

     d. underline important parts of the question, and be sure to answer all the parts

     e. prepare a brief outline of your answer

     f. write your answer and check off outline points as you write

     g. go to next easiest question and follow steps three to five and continue with the remaining questions

     h. spend the final 10 minutes reviewing your answers to detect and correct any errors in facts, grammar, or spelling

C. How you can use your past tests to improve your future test scores

  1. Pay very close attention to the questions you missed.

     a. does the correct answer surprise you, and if so, why

     b. where was the correct answer (book or lecture)

       i. did you highlight or underline it in your book

       ii. was it included in your notes

  2. Did you do as well as you thought you would

  3. Was there any type of question on which you did especially well

  4. Was there any type of question on which you did especially poorly and, if so, can you figure out why

  5. Change your method of study for each test until you find out what works best for you

D. The formula for maximizing test performance—Preparation + Control = Success

  1. Preparation before tests

      i. attend classes without fail

      ii. listen actively during lectures and take careful notes

      iii. use the SQ4R method to read assignments

      iv. divide study time into sections; do not cram

      v. study questions you missed on old tests so you can avoid missing them on future tests

      vi. review both alone and with others in the class, but remember that study sessions that are primarily social will not help your test scores

  2. Control during tests

     a. read all questions first

     b. ask your professor for clarification of questions

     c. answer the easiest questions first

     d. use the process of elimination (objective tests)

     e. outline answers (subjective tests

     f. review and check answers

  3. Success before, during, and after tests

     a. you will acquire, understand, and retain new and valuable knowledge

     b. you will achieve higher academic performance in the form of better grades

     c. you will increase your sense of self-esteem

Material learned in several short sessions is learned faster, retained longer, and understood better than the same amount of material learned in one long sitting. Therefore, avoid cramming.

Professors are particularly sensitive to the concept of academic honesty. Therefore, be sure that you are aware of all your instructor's rules for behavior during tests. Do not put yourself in the position of engaging in a behavior that a professor could perceive as academically dishonest.

Do not go into the first test in any class without having an idea of what it will be like. Therefore, try to find out about your professor's testing methods by asking students who have done well in the class before and examining old tests from the class if they are available.

Try to take tests in a relatively relaxed state of mind. Therefore, if you suffer from test anxiety, do something about it by visiting your college's counseling center. However, the best defense against test anxiety is adequate preparation. Most test anxiety is caused by the very realistic fear of failure that is the result of inadequate preparation.

Do not expect learning to be a quick and easy process. It will take time and sometimes it will be difficult. Expect to spend a minimum of 1.5 hours studying and writing papers, outside of class for each hour of class you attend. Therefore, think about college as a full-time job in which you must put in at least 40 hours of concentrated academic work per week (approximately 15 hours in class and another 24 hours of studying outside class). This still leaves you with 128 hours to eat, sleep, socialize, play, and relax each week!

Expect to be frustrated sometimes but do not give up just because something is hard to learn. You can succeed if you just make up your mind to do so!

USING THE <u>PUBLICATION MANUAL OF THE APA</u> FOR SUCCESSFUL ESSAY PAPER COMPLETION

When writing a paper for one of your courses, you will be required to complete the paper in the format specified by the <u>Publication Manual of the American Psychological Association 5th Edition (2002).</u> This is the definitive resource regarding the mechanics of writing a paper in psychology and other sciences. It provides detailed instruction and numerous examples regarding the correct formatting for acceptable written works. If you do not own a copy, this book can be found in the library and on the shelves of the department faculty. Again, any and all papers that you write for courses offered through the Psychology Department will require you to utilize the manual's format. Do not hesitate to ask for assistance should you need it.

Some highlights include:

1). Active vs. Passive Voice

The manual recommends the use of the active voice over the passive voice whenever possible. "The passive voice is acceptable in expository writing and when you want to focus on the object or recipient action rather than on the actor." The active voice is best as it serves as a direct communicator.

2). Past Tense

"Use [this] to express an action or a condition that occurred at a specific, definitive time in the past, as when discussing another researcher's work and when reporting your results."

3). Guidelines to reduce bias in language

Guideline 1: Describe to the appropriate level of specificity
Guideline 2: Be sensitive to labels
Guideline 3: Acknowledge participation

Issues along these lines are reflected through the following topic areas: gender, sexual orientation, racial and ethnic identity, disabilities, and age. Guidelines for unbiased language can be found on in the manual. This guideline offers a table which clearly outlines rules and examples (do's and don'ts) to avoid biases in language.

4). Page format

This section offers information regarding margins (1" for top, bottom, left, and right), line spacing (double), acceptable typefaces (times roman) and point sizes (12), and page numbering and header guidelines.

5) Citations in text

The manual offers many examples of citations in text. When referring to another person's work within your paper, that author must receive appropriate credit through the citation.

6). References

Once cited, the completed reference should appear in your reference/ bibliography section at the end of your paper. This section contains numerous examples of reference formats depending on the type of source.

For example:

A periodical would look like:

Silvin, M.H., & Jones, J.P. (1993). Test anxiety: Exploration as a personality trait. Journal of Personality and Social Psychology, 2 (3), 125-129.

An edited book would look like:
Gibbs, J.T., & Huang, L.N. (Eds.J). (1991). Children of color: Psychological interventions with minority youth. San Francisco: Jossey-Bass

A chapter in an edited book would look like:
Massaro, D. (1992). Boradening the domain of the fuzzy logical model of perception. In H.L. Pick, Jr., P. van den Broek, & D.C. Knill (Eds.), Cognition: Conceptual and methodological issues (pp. 51-84). Washington, DC: American Psychological Association.

TEACHING STUDENTS HOW TO LEARN THROUGH DISCUSSION

First, they need to understand the importance of discussion for learning. Expressing one's understanding or ideas and getting reactions from other students and the teacher makes a big difference in learning, retention, and use of knowledge.

A second attribute is the students' development of a willingness to talk about their own ideas openly and to listen and respond to others' ideas. It is important for students to realize that it is easy to deceive themselves about their own insights or understandings and that verbalizing an idea is one way of getting checks on and extensions of it. Teachers can encourage development of listening skills by asking one group member to repeat or paraphrase what another said before responding to it, and repeatedly pointing out the purpose and values students gain from discussion.

A third skill is planning. Discussions are sometimes frustrating because they are only getting under way when the end of the class period comes. If this results in continuation of the discussion outside the class, so much the better, but often learning is facilitated if students learn to formulate the issues and determine what out-of-class study or follow-up is necessary before the group breaks up.

A fourth skill is building on others' ideas in such a way as to increase their motivation rather than make them feel punished or forgotten. Often students see discussion as a competitive situation in which they win by tearing down other students' ideas. As Haines and McKeachie (1967) have shown, cooperative discussion methods encourage more effective work and better morale than competitive methods.

A fifth attribute is skill in evaluation. If classes are to learn how to discuss issues effectively, they need to review periodically what aspects of their discussion are proving to be worthwhile and what barriers, gaps, or difficulties have arisen. Some classes reserve the last five minutes of the period for a review of the discussion's effectiveness.. A sixth attribute is sensitivity to feelings of other group members. Students need to become aware of the possibility that feelings of rejection, frustration, dependence, and so on may influence group members' participation in discussion. Sometimes it is more productive to recognize the underlying feeling than to focus on the content of an individual's statement. One way of helping students develop these skills is to use student-led discussions preceded by a training meeting with the student leader.

HOW TO GET STUDENTS ACTIVELY THINKING IN A LECTURE SITUATION

As we have seen, a major problem with the lecture is that students assume a passive, nonthinking, information-receiving role. Yet, if they are to remember and use the information, they need to be actively engaged in thinking about the content presented. One easy and effective device is the "Minute Paper." The Minute Paper is, as its title indicates, a paper literally written in a minute (or it can be a two-minute or three-minute paper). Announce at the beginning of the class period that you will interrupt your lecture midway through the period so that the students may write a one-minute paper on a topic derived from the lecture or that you will ask them at the end of the lecture to write the most important thing they have learned. Even better, you can ask them also to write the most important thing they learned from the previous week's lecture.

You ordinarily will want a discussion to be a dialog about the complexity of the issue, the fact that there are pros and cons for each position, and perhaps that a resolution may be found other than a decision for one position and against the other.

So now, where do you start to apply all of this good information? Get organized!

Despite our best efforts and intentions, success alludes us. With the behavior of successful academic outcome, research findings from application of learning theory have identified some successful predictors.

Whether you select a Palm Pilot$^©$, Daytimer$^©$, or index cards in your pocket, plan your day and your studies. Chart your workload for all assignments and examinations. Match parallel to this listing how these activities fit into your goals for majoring in Psychology. For example, save all of your work–No, not to use again but to refer and possibly put together in a portfolio for a job, or graduate school application. The following strategies have been identified as good predictors of successful academic performance. Review them, consider what you do now and try a new strategy for at least one week to see if you can change your outcomes.

Consider this as an investment into yourself that you will benefit from over the rest of your lifetime. An academic experience, education is just that. So you see that the process of education, taken in a large way, may be described as nothing but the process of acquiring ideas or conceptions, the best educated mind being the mind which has the largest stock of them, ready to meet the largest possible variety of the emergencies of life.

Chapter 3

Advising

HOW DO YOU SPELL RELIEF? THE ACADEMIC ADVISING SYSTEM

"I have to meet with my adviser so I can register for my classes." This statement unfortunately reflects the limited perspective on what advising can offer. Many times students, and some faculty, see advising as no more than a place to complete paper work in order to register for the next term's courses. Yes, advising is a means through which registration of courses occurs, but it can be so much more if given the chance.

ADVISING AS MENTORSHIP

Your adviser is a faculty member who also contributes to the field of psychology through research, publication, consultation, and service provision. This is a person with a wealth of knowledge and experience that stretches beyond the registration documents. Students can use the advising session as a means to tap into that resource.

Ask questions about yourself:
- What are my strengths?
- What are my challenges?
- What are the aspects of psychology that excite me?
- What type of populations am I interested in?
- What type of work settings excite me?
- What is my motivation to pursue the field of psychology?
- What is my dedication to the study of psychology?

Ask questions about your adviser:
- What made you choose psychology as your career?
- What types of experiences did you have as an undergraduate?
- What type of mentor did you have?
- What advise can you offer to help me navigate through graduate school admissions procedures?
- What advice can you give me to help with my career goals?

Your advisor may be able to connect you with people in the field who can serve as an additional resource. Your adviser is also available to meet with you throughout the year to offer guidance and suggestions regarding your academic progress, career goals, and graduate school interests.

ADVISING AS A MEANS TO GRADUATE SCHOOL AND A CAREER

Psychology programs at the undergraduate level offer a wide variety of courses designed to provide exposure to the breadth of the field. There are core courses you must take to meet the requirements of the major that will vary slightly from program to program. The core courses are a pathway that faculty have designed for students. A close inspection of the psychology electives reveals that one can select from them and design a track that best enhances one's area of future study or career ideals. Undergraduate students interested in clinical or counseling psychology, for example, would be advised to take electives such as "Psychological Tests and Measurements", "Personality Theory," "Introduction to Clinical/Counseling Psychology," and "Abnormal Psychology" just to name a few. An interest in industrial/organizational psychology would best be met by such electives as "Motivation," "Introduction to I/O Psychology," and "Personality Theory." Reflective conversations with one's adviser is the means to selecting the courses that best meet your interest and future goals. Your advisor can also provide suggestions of how other disciplines of study at your institution offer courses that could enhance your development. As an example, it is often helpful for students interested in working with youth offenders to also take courses offered in a criminal justice program (e.g., juvenile justice, the criminal justice system). The correct blend of courses both within and outside of the major can enhance one's transcript and knowledge-base thereby making one a more attractive job and graduate school applicant.

In addition, some institutions offer courses every other year. This is important to know if you are trying to develop your electives into a tract. You do not want to miss out on an important class just because you never articulated your goals to your adviser. **YOU NEED TO BE CONSCIOUS AND INFORMED OF THE SCHOOL COLLEGE CATALOG.**

THE ADVISING SESSION

It is to your advantage to make your appointment early in the advising period as designated by your institution. The benefit is twofold: (1) securing your advising appointment at convenient times, and (2) optimizing your changes for getting the course you want before they are closed out. It is important that you present to the advising appointment prepared. Bring your course catalog and registration materials. It is important that you be familiar with how to read the catalog and are familiar with the course offerings in your major. Have a general idea of the courses you with to take. Be ready to discuss your goals and objectives. Your adviser will ask you questions to clarify your ideas and thereby offer you the best advise.

Major Entry #3

List ten things you want to do/cover in your next advising appointment.

What questions do you have about the psychology courses you are interested in taking?

Course   Question

1)

2)

3)

4)

THE ADVISER-ADVISEE RELATIONSHIP

The adviser-advisee relationship carries certain expectations from both participants. What follows is a list of responsibilities and expectations related to both members of this dyad.

Faculty Adviser Responsibilities:
- To be dedicated to the advising process as a human, caring relationship.
- To strive to be accessible to students.
- To encourage students in self-direction and understanding of personal responsibilities as advisees.
- To assist students in achieving academic, career, and personal goals.
- To assist students in selecting course that reflect individual interests and abilities.
- To be familiar with graduation requirements and other institutional policies outlined by the institution.
- To understand the division of responsibilities and authorities between student, adviser, department, and college/university.
- To refer students to appropriate campus resources.

Student Advisee Responsibilities:
- Recognize that advising is a shared responsibility, but also realize that the student is ultimately responsible for making decisions regarding academic, career, and personal goals.
- Are responsible for preparing for and keeping appointments with the adviser.
- Develop plans for achieving academic, career, and personal goals.
- Maintain updated check-sheets and develop plans for taking course required for graduation.
- Be familiar with graduation requirements and other institutional policies as outlined in your institution's catalog.
- Make use of the full range of campus resources.

Calculating Your Grade-Point Average (GPA) (But I Thought I Was Magna Cum Laude)

The following outline provides the steps to follow for calculating your grade-point average (GPA). An example has also been provided to help clarify the steps.

1. List each course with the number of credits and the course grade:

Course	Credits	Grade
EDU 100	.50	B
BIO 104	1.00	D
PED 100	.25	P
POL 210	1.00	B
ENG 106	1.00	A
PSY 100	1.00	C

2. Multiply the number of credits in each course by the number of grade points corresponding with your letter grade:

Grade Points (Gps)

A = 4.0 pts.   *Note: P/NP and AU are not used to calculate grade points.*
B = 3.0 pts.
C = 2.0 pts.
D = 1.0 pts.
F = 0.0 pts.

Course	Credits	Grade	Points	Gps
EDU 100	.50	B	3	.50 x 3 = 1.5
BIO 104	1.00	D	1	1.00 x 1 = 1.0
PED 100	.25	P	0	none
POL 210	1.00	B	3	1.00 x 3 = 3.0
ENG 106	1.00	A	4	1.00 x 4 = 1.0
PSY 100	1.00	C	2	1.00 x 2 = 2.0

3. Add the credits and the grade points for every course in which a letter grade was received:

Course	Credits	Gps
EDU 100	.50	1.5
BIO 104	1.00	1.0
POL 210	1.00	3.0
ENG 106	1.00	4.0

PSY 100	<u>1.00</u>	<u>1.0</u>
	4.50	11.5

4. Divide the number of grade points by the number of credits for the semester:
   Credits = 4.5; GPS = 11.5
   GPS ÷ Credits = GPA
   11.5 ÷ 4.50 = 2.55 (GPA)

PSYCHOLOGY CLASSES OFFERED AT VARIOUS COLLEGES

We conducted a survey of the Chicago region psychology curriculum and our results had considerable variation of course titles for content area. We have categorized 11 major areas and list the corresponding course titles. We've listed our findings below. How is the Psychology major at your college organized?

Introductory

General Psychology/Intro to Psychology
Psychology: Science of Behavior
Psychology Lab
Survey of Psychology

Developmental/Lifespan

Child and Adolescent Development
Childhood and Adolescence
Developmental Psychology: Infancy and Early Childhood
Developmental Psychology: Middle Childhood
Developmental Psychology: Adolescence
Adolescence and Youth
Adolescent Development and Learning
Adolescence and the Transition to Adulthood
Adolescent and Adult Developmental Psychology
Infancy & Childhood
Infant, Child & Adolescent Psychology
Early Childhood Growth and Development
Child Developmental Psychology
Adult Development and Aging
Aging
Adult Development
Adult Learning and Portfolio

Developmental Psychology: Adulthood
Developmental Psychology
Survey of the Exceptional Child
Advanced Study of Psychology of Children with Exceptionalities
Psychology of Children with Exceptionalities
Psychology and Methods of Teaching the Exceptional Learner
Survey of Exceptional Children and Adolescence
Psychological Diagnosis of Exceptional Children
Exceptional Child
Exceptional individual
Affective Education in Middle Schools
Death and Dying
Lifespan Development
Human Development through the Life Cycle
Human Growth and Development
Social Gerontology

Biological/Physiological

Sensation and Perception
Sensation and Perception Lab
Perception
Physiological Psychology
Physiological Psychology Lab
Psychobiology
Biopsychology

Social/Applied Industrial Organizational

Career and Life Planning
Career and Management
Careers in Psychology
Employment Strategies for Arts &
    Science & Nursing Students
Industrial/Organizational psychology
Organizational Psychology
Industrial Psychology
Organizational Training

Readings in Organizational Research
Organizational Behavior
Social Psychology
Persuasion
Personnel
Psychology of Human Communication
Consumer Behavior
Organizational Motivation

Abnormal/Applied Clinical

Personality
Theories of Personality and
    Development
Personality Theory and Research
Personality: Theory and Therapy
Personality laboratory
Advanced Personality Theories
Counseling the Elderly
Principles of Counseling
Theories of Counseling
Counseling Psychology
Counseling Skills
Counseling in the Helping Professions
Counseling Practicum
Marriage and Family Counseling
Individual and Group Counseling
Intro to Counseling
Children with Mental Retardation
Students with Learning Disabilities
Behavior Management
Behavior Modification/Lab
Behavior Assessment and management
Human Behavior and the Social
    Environment
Group Processes
Group Theory and Leadership

Group Therapy
Individual and Group Dynamics
Introduction to the Study of Psychopathology
Psychopathology
Advanced Psychopathology
Child and Adolescent Psychopathology
Psychopathology of the Child
Psychotherapy
Psychotherapeutic Techniques
Theories of Psychotherapy
Intro to Clinical Psychology
Contemporary Clinical Psychology
Marriage and the Family
Crisis Intervention
Interpersonal Relations
Basic Helping Skills
The Psychology of Personal Growth
The Nature of Persons
Psychology of Adjustment and Growth
Group Dynamics
Health Psychology

Research/Statistics/Applied Research

Basic Research and Statistics
Advanced Research and Statistics
Statistics
Statistics for the Behavioral Sciences
Applied Behavior Analysis
Experimental Psychology
Experimental Psychology II
Experimental Research Project
Experimental Design
Psychological Testing
Psychological Testing and Evaluation
Psychological Testing and Educational
    Tests and Measurements

Psychological Tests & Measurements
Psychometrics and Assessments
Survey of Psychological Assessment
Basic Research Skills
Methods of Research
Research in Psychology
Research Method in the Social Sciences
Basic Approaches to Psychological Research
Advanced Design and Research
Research Experience
Research Design & Experimentation

Learning, Cognition, Motivation, Memory

Learning and Behavior Modification
Theories of Learning
Learning and Cognition
Learning and Cognition Lab
Cognitive Process
Cognition
Motivation
Human Learning and Memory

Conditioning and Learning
Learning Theory and Application
Cognitive Psychology
Cerebral Effects of Consciousness
Cerebral Effects of Consciousness Lab
Educational Psychology
Thought and Language

Field Experience, Practicum, Internship

Practicum in Clinical/Counseling
   Psychology
Clinical Practicum/Lab
Practicum in Organizational
   Psychology
Practicum in Crisis Intervention
Practicum in Teaching Psychology
Research Practicum
Research Mentorship

Supervised Field Education
Field Placement
Field Work in Psychology
Psychology Practicum
Internship in Human Resource
   Management
Internship in Psychology
Independent Research in Psychology

Specialty Courses

Alcohol Problems and Alcoholism
Substance Abuse
Intro to Chemical Dependency
Drugs and Behavior
Women in Contemporary Society
Psychology of Women
Psychology of the Family
Psychology of Religious Behavior
Psychology and Religion
The Interface between Psychology and
   Christianity

Integration of Psychology and Christianity
Psychology of Religion
Psychology of Morality
Sport Psychology
Psychology and Contemporary Mysticism
Methods in the Integration of Psychology
   and Theology
Teaching Psychology in Secondary Schools
Psychology and Literature
Computers for the Social Sciences

Diversity

Gender Roles
Gender, Self, and Society
Psychology of Gender
Psychology of Sexual Differences
Interpersonal Relationships
Sexuality in Human Experience

Human Sexuality
Community Psychology
South Africa, Racism and Leadership
Cross Cultural Psychology
Personal Lives and Social World

History of Psychology/Selected Topics Seminar

History of Psychology
History and Systems of Psychology
Special Topics
Selected Topics
Contemporary Issues in Psychology
Current Applications in Psychology
Systems and Theories
Readings in Psychology
Psychology Research Seminar

Departmental Honors in Psychology
Honors Thesis
Seminar
Senior Seminar in Psychology
Senior Thesis
Independent Study
Topics
Directed Study

Chapter 4

Careers

WHAT WAS YOUR DEGREE IN??? PUTTING YOUR LIBERAL ARTS SKILLS TO WORK

Undergraduate college students often overlook the relevance of their liberal arts education to the world of work. While the primary purpose of a university or college is to provide its students with a well-rounded education—rather than training them for one specific job—many of the skills developed in the classroom have direct bearing on success in the workplace. Throughout their undergraduate years, students are required to develop and refine their writing, speaking and research skills. These skills are fundamental to career success. Part of what distinguishes liberal arts education is its breadth of exposure to different disciplines. Students must learn to write and speak clearly about and conduct scholarly research on topics outside their majors. The ability to adapt to different environments, to understand viewpoints different from their own, and to comprehend unfamiliar information is important in may careers and essential to job advancement (e.g., promotions and raises). Another advantage of a liberal arts education is that, because classes are small, students are often assigned projects requiring them to develop and improve their writing, speaking, and research skills. Your peers at larger institutions seldom have the opportunity to give in-class presentations or to receive comments about the style and content of their writing assignments. Undergraduate students often underestimate the value of their education and their opportunities to develop job-related skills and, because of this, they are also often unable to sell their skills to potential employers. To become aware of the skills you are developing, reflect on the assignments you have completed in your classes and use the following lists to compare what you are acquiring with what will be expected of you in your future job.

WRITING SKILLS

In College➜➜ ➜➜➜➜➜

♦ term papers and essay tests
♦ laboratory
♦ peer reviewing
♦ notebooks and journa
♦ creative writing

On the Job

♦ writing reports, briefs, and proposals
♦ composition letters and memos
♦ editing and proofreading
♦ keeping clear and accurate records
♦ preparing copy for sales, advertising and publications

SPEAKING SKILLS

In College➜➜ ➜➜➜➜➜

♦ speeches and presentations
♦ study groups
♦ discussions and debates
♦ group projects

♦ answering questions in class

On the Job

♦ interviewing, supervising, counseling
♦ persuading, negotiating, and selling
♦ making presentations to peers/clients
♦ surveying and soliciting funds and support
♦ working with the public and answering their questions

RESEARCH SKILLS

In College➜➜ ➜➜➜➜➜

♦ library and laboratory research
♦ independent studies
♦ co-op or internship projects
♦ literature review

♦ case studies

On the Job

♦ planning and decision making
♦ developing ideas and brainstorming
♦ designing and conducting research
♦ gathering, analyzing, and interpreting data
♦ developing programs and market plans

These are only a few of the skills developed in the classroom that have direct on-the-job application. Colleges/universities also provide numerous extracurricular opportunities for students to develop other career-related skills (e.g., leadership and problem-solving). Students should use the following three-part strategy to prepare themselves for success in today's increasingly competitive job market.

❶ Become aware of the skills you will need to obtain and succeed in the job to which you aspire.
❷ Take full advantage of the opportunities provided to enable you to develop these skills
❸ Make prospective employers aware of your skills (e.g., learn how to write an effective resume, develop persuasive interviewing skills).

WHAT DO EMPLOYERS LOOK FOR IN A PSYCHOLOGY MAJOR INTERVIEWING FOR A JOB?

The items in the three major categories of the following outline (taken directly from Edwards & Smith, 1988) are arranged in descending order of importance as rated by a large sample of employers from Midwestern government, nonprofit, and commercial agencies, organizations, and companies that often hire undergraduate psychology majors. Psychology students are urged to take advantage of all their undergraduate opportunities to maximize the attainments of these skills, abilities, knowledge, and personal traits.

SKILLS AND ABILITIES

- Writing proposals and reports
- Identifying and solving problems based on research and knowledge of behavior
- Conducting interviews
- Performing statistical analyses
- Designing and conducting research projects
- Performing job analyses
- Coding data
- Using computer programs to analyze data
- Systematically observing and recording behavior
- Constructing tests and questionnaires
- Administering standardized tests

KNOWLEDGE

- Formation and change of attitudes and opinions
- Principles and techniques of personnel selection
- How people think, solve problems, and process information
- Structure and dynamics of small groups
- Effects of the environment on people's feelings and actions
- Organizational development
- Principles of human learning and memory
- How people perceive and sense their environment
- Theories and research on personality and individual differences
- Principles of human needs and motivation

📕 Theories and research on organizational behavior, work, and productivity
📕 Theories and research on human development and stages of life
📕 Symptoms, causes, and treatments of abnormal behaviors

PERSONAL TRAITS

🤚 Ability to work with others in a team
🤚 Motivation to work hard
🤚 Positive attitude toward work and the organization
🤚 Organization
🤚 Leadership
🤚 Maturity
🤚 Flexibility
🤚 Ability to communicate well
🤚 Intelligence
🤚 Problem-solving ability
🤚 Integrity
🤚 Tolerance for stress and ambiguity

WRITING A GOOD RESUME
YOU ARE THE PRODUCT—ADVERTISE YOURSELF

You will need a resume or some type of data sheet when applying for field experiences and it can be updated as you accomplish more. Obviously, you will use it for your job application procedure once you finish your Psychology degree.

The resume is a concise synopsis of your accomplishments. It is important that your resume be "lean and mean." Truth is—most employers/committees will not give it a thorough reading. The individual who reviews your resume for a job or application is a busy person. You want to give him/her an accurate and thorough run-through of your accomplishments in as precise and condensed a fashion as possible. Therefore, it is important that you hit the most important areas of your background in a clear manner. Keep in mind that a resume is not only useful for your job search, but is also a tool you want to use when applying to graduate schools.

When building a resume, one must focus on the organization. Keep in mind that there is no "right or wrong" way to organize your resume. Your goal is to organize it so it makes the most sense to the busy reader. What follows is a generic format for resume construction.

1. At the top of the page, you should have your name (preferably in bold lettering) and your home address and phone number. If you wish to include your work phone number, do so here. For example:

Resume
Mary Smith
1234 Main Street
Peoria, IL 60126
(home) 323-123-4467
(work) 323-987-6543

2. **Education** List your major and minor areas of study, the school, and the years of attendance or the year of graduation. For example:

Education
1993-Present BS Psychology—Great College, Peoria, IL

OR

January 1988 BS Psychology—Great College, Peoria, IL

3. **Employment.** List your job title, employer, years of employment, and your job responsibilities. Some people choose to bullet their job responsibilities, others write them in paragraph form. It's up to you to choose the method you feel works best. When writing the content be consistent. Always start your points with an action verb and do not use statements such as "I did.." Prioritize the content so that the most important job function is the first one listed. For example:

Employment
1988–1989 <u>Child Care Specialist.</u> Fun time Day Care for Disabled Children, Peoria, IL
   - Served as a classroom activity facilitator for parent training classes.
   - Coordinated daily activities for 0-3 year old children.
   - Worked with a population of children with a variety of disorders including Autism, Oppositional Defiant Disorder, and Attention Deficit/Hyperactivity Disorder.

OR

<u>1988-1989</u> <u>Child Care Specialist.</u> Fun Time Day Care for Disabled Children, Peoria, IL Served as a classroom activity facilitator for parent training classes. Coordinated daily activities for 0-3 year old children. Worked with a population of children with a variety of disorders including Autism, Oppositional Defiant Disorder, and Attention Deficit/Hyperactivity Disorder.

If you have volunteer experiences, you want to represent them in their own section following the employment section. It's important to distinguish between paid positions and those you did as a volunteer. The section heading is simply "<u>Service Experiences</u>" and follows the same format described above.

4. **Honors.** If you have received any honors (e.g., Dean's list, Employee of the Year) list them here. You want to shine by displaying achievements that may place you ahead of other job or graduate school applicants. For example:

1996   Volunteer of the Year, Memorial Hospital, Peoria, IL

1988   Dean's List, Great College, Peoria, IL

5. **Publications and Presentations**. If you are lucky enough to have been awarded authorship on a presentation or publication, make sure you include it in the appropriate section. The <u>APA Style Manual</u> (2002) provides information on how to correctly write the content of these sections. Put your publications under a <u>Publications</u> section and your presentations under a <u>Presentations</u> section. For example:

<u>Publications</u>
Smith, J., & Jones, K. (1994). The use of medication versus relaxation training on test anxiety. <u>Journal of Test Anxiety, 32</u> (3), 123-127.

<u>Presentations</u>
Smith, J., & Jones, K. (1993). <u>The effectiveness of relaxation training on test anxiety.</u> Poster presented to the American Association for Test Anxiety Convention, Chicago, Illinois.

6. **Current Research** As a student, you may be currently involved in a research protocol that has not yet been presented or published. You definitely want to represent on your resume that you are actively involved in on-going projects. To that end, you will want to include a section about your current research involvement. For example: Smith, J., & Jones, K., <u>A proposed measure for test anxiety in undergraduate students taking statistics courses.</u>

7. **Professional Memberships** To belong to professional organizations in the field of psychology further shows your interest in the field. Organizations, such as the American Psychological Association and American Psychological Society, have reduced rates for student members. Many organizations exist within the different specialty areas in psychology. As a member of most organizations, you receive the organization journal, newspaper, and other relevant information about the field. These should also be represented on your resume.

You may want to include other sections in your resume to represent your background. The Office of Career Planning and Development at your college/university can provide additional information regarding resume construction. You can meet one-on-one with a representative or attend one of the many workshops they provide to students such as yourself.

Most importantly, <u>do not pad your resume</u>. Be truthful about your experiences and represent them accurately. Employers and graduate school selection committees will check to see if what you have indicated is accurate.

A typical resume is not usually more than two pages. As your resume becomes more detailed, you will want to change the heading to a "curriculum vita." The major difference between a resume and curriculum vitae is the level of detail. More information on the curriculum vitae can be provided by your faculty advisor.

CAREERS IN PSYCHOLOGY

Some psychology majors enter the world of work immediately after graduation, while others continue their education to prepare for more specialized employment. This chapter will help both groups prepare for, obtain, and succeed in the careers to which they aspire.

The Following section will provide you with the following information:

1). employment opportunities/strategies,
2). an employment-planning time-line for the student with a bachelors degree in psychology,
3). advice for successful employment in the 21st century,
4). explanation regarding the value of a liberal arts education for career preparation,
5). description of job-related skills acquired by psychology majors that are valued by prospective employers.

In addition, this chapter explains how and where baccalaureate psychology graduates and master's and doctorally prepared psychologists are employed, and the range of salaries they receive. To that end, the first portion of this chapter is dedicated to the student looking for employment with a baccalaureate degree in psychology, while the last portion provides information for those interested in pursuing a career after graduate school.

EMPLOYMENT OPPORTUNITIES AND STATEGIES FOR INDIVIDUALS WITH A BACHELORS DEGREE IN PSYCHOLOGY...

A simple response to the question, "What can I do with a major in psychology?" might be, "just about anything that involves working with people." Another approach would be to list all of the occupations that psychology majors have successfully pursued. Neither of these approaches by itself, however, helps **YOU** to make career decisions. The purpose of this section is, not only to provide you with some information about potential employment opportunities after completing your psychology degree, but also to make some suggestions about how to handle occupational decisions and successfully land that first job.

Let us begin with some important facts. The undergraduate major in psychology is a LIBERAL ARTS DEGREE, not a professional degree. It does not make you a psychologist or a professional counselor. These occupations require specific training at the graduate level and are regulated by state and federal law. If such occupations interest you, be prepared to continue your education in graduate school.

While some occupations in psychology require graduate training, there are many interesting and rewarding career opportunities available to the individuals with a bachelors degree in psychology. You selection of an appropriate occupation, however, requires some self-analysis and research. Ultimately, successful employment depends on your efforts to:

1). make informed decisions about your career,
2). learn about prospective occupations,
3). acquire appropriate knowledge, skills, and characteristics,
4). learn how to conduct a well-planned job search.

This section will address each of these four points.

Major Entry #4

What are my short term and long term career goals?

SHORT TERM	LONG TERM
1.	1.
2.	2.
3.	3.
4.	4.
5.	5.

Making Informed Decisions About Your Career

An occupational choice can be one of the most difficult decisions a person makes, with consequences for both life satisfaction and life style. Unfortunately, many students approach this decision in a haphazard and informal manner; they neither explore potential occupations systematically nor prepare themselves adequately to successfully obtain a particular job. In fact, many students simply do not worry about careers until their senior year, when they discover that they lack courses or have failed to develop necessary skills for occupations that interest them.

Successful career planning requires careful and objective self-assessment, a realistic understanding of your aptitudes and skills, an awareness of responsibilities associated with potential employment settings, careful selection of experiences designed to develop marketable skills and knowledge, and an action plan for conducting a successful job search. The following sections are designed to give you some guidance in each area.

Self-Assessment

Socrates said, "Know thyself." Two thousand years later, this is still good advice. It is essential that you know (or discover) your interests, preferences, values, aptitudes, and abilities. There are several formal opportunities. Many campuses offer direction and guidance through a career services office often are free. A career counselor can assist you through a formal interview and completion of various vocational interest inventories. In addition, there are several helpful computerized tools designed to provide the user with valuable information about various careers. Discussions with faculty (e.g., advisor, mentor) can help you reflect on career goals as well as provide you with additional contacts for help to further clarify your needs. Look through your course catalog and see if courses in career development are offered. Some psychology departments offer a "Careers in Psychology" course where guest speakers lecture on their specific area.

Learning About Prospective Occupations

Surveys of employers and psychology graduates indicate that the jobs obtained by psychology majors with a bachelors degree are most often in social service and business settings, such as:

<u>Business:</u> *personnel administrator, loan officer, retail sales management, occupational analyst, industrial relations specialist, claims specialist, and marketing representative.*

<u>Social Services:</u> *group home attendant, case worker, probation officer, admissions counselor, occupational therapist, substance abuse counselor, youth counselor, employment counselor, social service aid, public health administrator, parole officer, social-urban planner, community relations officer, affirmative action officer, vocational rehabilitation, and day care center supervisor.*

Acquiring Appropriate Knowledge, Skills and Characteristics

Part of knowing and marketing yourself involves a clear understanding of the specific knowledge, skills, and characteristics (KSCs) valued by employers and obtained through completing the bachelors degree in psychology. Numerous studies have documented the KSCs employers look for in prospective employees, and they are summarized in the following lists. Psychology courses that emphasize specific skills or types of knowledge are indicated in parentheses. It is important that you develop and communicate your proficiency in these KSCs to be successful in the job market.

Knowledge Learned by Psychology Majors That Employers Seek

☺ How attitudes and opinions are formed and changed (Social Psychology)
☺ Principles and techniques of personal selection and organizational development (Industrial Psychology)
☺ How people think, solve problems and process information (Human Information Processing)
☺ Structure and dynamics of small groups (Social Psychology)
☺ Effects of environment on people's feelings and actions (Psychology of Motivation)
☺ Principles of human learning and memory (Psychology of Learning)

Skills Learned By Psychology Majors Who Employers Seek

☺ Identifies and solves problems based upon a knowledge of research methodology and understanding of human behavior (General Psychology and Experimental Methods in Psychology.
☺ Performs statistical analyses (Statistical Methods)
☺ Designs and conducts research projects (Directed Research in Psychology)
☺ Selects, administers, and interprets psychological tests (Psychological Tests and Measurement)
☺ Gathers and organizes information from multiple sources (Senior Seminar)
☺ Works productively as a member of a team (History and Systems of Psychology)
☺ Plans and carries out projects successfully (Independent Study)
☺ Ability to manage stress (Stress Management)
☺ Conducts interviews (Clinical Psychology)
☺ Writes proposals and reports (any psychology class that requires a paper)

☺ Speaks articulately and persuasively (any psychology class that requires an oral presentation)

Characteristics Rated Highly by Employers

☺ Satisfactory grades
☺ Strong communication and interpersonal skills
☺ Outgoing personality
☺ Ability to present oneself in a positive manner
☺ Relevant previous employment
☺ Enthusiasm
☺ Flexibility
☺ Leadership
☺ Problem solving abilities
☺ High energy level
☺ Maturity

As you can see, many of the skills listed above are important components of the psychology curriculum. In fact, the core of courses that all psychology majors take emphasizes skill development in all of these areas. When it comes to content areas in psychology, however, it is important to carefully select courses that best match your potential career.

Another important, yet often overlooked, aspect of skill and knowledge development is your selection of elective courses and a minor. For example, many graduates with a bachelors degree in psychology are employed in business settings. Therefore, it would be wise to consider taking some business courses. Courses offered by other departments can be essential in obtaining job skills and knowledge for your future occupation as well. These courses can be used as electives or applied to a minor. Once you have narrowed down your potential employment settings, you should meet with your advisor to discuss the best selection of courses to help you obtain your career objective.

Potential employers also value some practical experience. There are several options to obtain this experience. One strategy is to seek part-time jobs related to your desired employment setting. Service learning options, field work/internship placements, and volunteer experiences are also a means through which one can gain employment. In some cases, agencies are more willing to hire someone after they have directly experienced the quality of their work. These experiences can also provide you with networking opportunities important for securing positions at other locations/agencies.

Conducting a Well-Planned Job Search

By the beginning of your senior year, you should have decided on a career path and obtained the basic skills and knowledge necessary for an entry position in that field. Unfortunately, your future employers will not seek you out; you will have to aggressively seek out and convince them that YOU are the employee that they should hire. To accomplish this: 1) identify position openings and make contacts, 2) develop an effective resume, 3) learn to interview successfully some strategies for each of these are discussed below. However, your best resource for all aspects of preparing to get your first job is the career placement office.

Identifying Potential Job Openings

The Career Placement Office is your primary resource in your search for potential jobs, but here are several other strategies for identifying potential job openings. First, ask people you know to identify individuals with whom you might talk to about your career interest. Friends, family, past or present employers, and people with whom you have done volunteer work are all excellent resources for contacts. Another strategy is to use the yellow pages of the phone book to identify companies, agencies or organizations that may employ people in your career interest area. Call these companies or agencies and ask to speak to a person who holds the type of position that you are seeking.

When you contact someone, explain that you are an undergraduate student nearing graduation and that you are interested in obtaining a job in their profession. Ask if they would be available to meet with you for an "information interview" to discuss their profession. The worst that can happen is that they will say "no". Be prepared to offer them several potential meeting times. Do not attempt to conduct the interview on the phone at that monument. The person may be busy and only able to give you cursory information. Be sure you go to the interview with a list of well thought-out questions. Toward the end of the interview, ask if they can suggest other people to talk to about the profession. This helps expand your contacts.

Finally, another source of job openings is the newspaper. Every day numerous jobs are listed under headings such as administrative assistant, customer service, sales, day care, and management—all of which are potential career options with your psychology degree. Read the job descriptions in advertisements very carefully, or you may miss a good potential opportunity. For example, there was a recent advertisement for a "resident manager" in the Sunday edition of the Indianapolis Star. Although you may have quickly skipped over this, the advertisement was seeking a resident manager for a girl's group home, a job relevant for career interest in social services.

Developing an Effective Resume

Your resume is a critical element of an effective job search. It may be the only initial contact you have with a potential employer. In other situations, your resume is the only record the employer has after the interview. An effective resume is neat, easily read, and provides a concise summary of your professional goals, education, and experience. You may even want to develop more than one resume for different occupational goals. Begin working on your resume during the summer prior to graduation. This allows plenty of time to get feedback on your resume (from your advisor and Career Placement Office) and to revise it as

The Job Interview

Your interview with prospective employer is your opportunity to impress them with your potential as a future employee. Although few initial interviews result in an immediate job offer, the first interview plays a crucial role in identifying candidates that the company may look at more closely. Therefore, it is critical that you make a strong, favorable first impression. The most important personal qualities that employers look for are good communication skills, clearly defined professional goals, and an honest outgoing personality.

Take interviews very seriously and prepare for each one in advance. Make an appointment with one of the psychology faculty to do a video-taped practice interview. In addition, be knowledgeable about the employer with whom you are interviewing. This will enable you to ask specific questions about the company that will generate a favorable impression. Finally, follow up the interview with a thank-you note. This reinforces the favorable impression you made during the interview and keeps you fresh in the interviewer's mind. Portions of this section were adapted from Handbook of Kennesaw State College Psychology Department Handbook (Hill, 1992) and Career Development and Opportunities for Psychology Majors Ware, 1993).

HOW ARE PSYCHOLOGISTS EMPLOYED?

A graduate education in psychology prepares individuals for a remarkable range of employment opportunities. According to Wise (1987), psychologists are employed in the five following major roles, but it is important to realize that many psychologists perform in more than one of these roles (e.g., the college teacher who counsels students, performs research, consults with other teachers to improve their testing procedures, and acts as the chairman of the department). The career paths that psychologists take are dependent upon their levels of education and their areas of interest.

TEACHING

Psychologists teach in two-and four-year colleges, and universities

RESEARCH

Psychologists are employed by universities, government agencies, the military, and businesses to conduct basic and applied studies of human behavior

PROVIDING SERVICES

Psychologists work with people of all ages and backgrounds who are coping with every
imaginable kind of problem, by assessing their needs and providing appropriate treatment

ADMINISTRATION

Psychologists work as managers in hospitals, mental health clinics, nonprofit organizations, government agencies, schools, universities, and businesses.

CONSULTING

Psychologists with expertise in a variety of areas are hired by organizations to provide
Consultative services on subject or problem if the consultant is an expert. These services
Can include designing a marketing survey and organizing outpatient mental health services."

WHERE ARE PSYCHOLOGY MAJORS EMPLOYED AND HOW DOES A LIBERAL ARTS EDUCATION HELP GRADUATES IN THEIR CAREERS?

A report from the National Science Foundation (1986) on employed bachelors-level graduates in psychology revealed that the following percentages were employed in five major areas one year after graduation

50%	Business and industry
27%	Science and engineering
15%	Educational institutions
10%	Nonprofit organizations
8%	Federal, state, or local government

The work that these graduates performed in these various areas included the following broad range of areas, skills, and responsibilities.

30%	Management
28%	Sales and professional services
16%	Teaching
12%	Production and inspection
14%	Other

These data clearly demonstrate that students who graduate with a psychology major are versatile individuals capable of gaining and maintaining meaningful employment in many different career areas.

More than 2,000 graduates of the University of Virginia recently identified the following five skills as critical factors in their current job success (Benner & Hitchcock, 1986). More than 91% of the respondents in this study confirmed the value of a liberal arts education as the best preparation for their current careers.

Oral Communication—presenting ideas to others orally, both one-on-one and in groups
Written Communication—writing effective letters, reports, and other documents

Interpersonal—understanding and dealing effectively with the behavior of others

Critical Thinking—identifying and analyzing problems, formulating and testing ideas

Problem solving—thinking and solving problems effectively

These are the same skills that psychology majors can master if they take full advantage of the curricular and extracurricular opportunities that are available to them at their colleges. It is important to note that many of those surveyed by Benner and Hitchcock were employed in areas not normally associated with the liberal arts, but it was the broad skills of a liberally educated person that helped them to succeed in their professions instead of the technical methods or information they gained in their specific disciplines (e.g., accounting or business.

EMPLOYMENT OPPORTUNITIES FOR PSYCHOLOGISTS

The Occupational Outlook Handbook is a wonderful source of information for undergraduates. It provides valuable information about occupational choices. The information in the sections which follow is taken verbatim with minor additions from the psychology section of the 1994-1995 edition of this publication. In addition, the description of 15 specialty areas in psychology (from APA's Careers in Psychology booklet) has been integrated into this information.

Psychologists study human behavior and mental processes to describe, understand, predict, and change people's behavior. They may study the way a person thinks, feels or behaves. Research psychologists investigate the physical, cognitive, emotional, or social aspects of human behavior. Psychologists in applied fields counsel and conduct graining programs; do market research; apply psychological treatments to a variety of medical and surgical conditions; or provide mental health services in hospitals, clinics, or private settings.

Like other social scientists, psychologists formulate hypotheses and collect data to test their validity. Research methods depend on the topic under study. Psychologists may gather information through controlled laboratory experiments; personality, performance, aptitude, and intelligence tests; observation, interviews, and questionnaires; clinical studies; or surveys. Computers are widely used to record and analyze this information.

Since psychology deals with human behavior, psychologists apply their knowledge and techniques to a wise range of endeavors including human services, management, education, law and sports. In addition to the variety of work settings, psychologists specialize in many different areas. Graduate education is a process of further refinement during which students become increasingly more proficient in and knowledgeable of an area of psychological specialization. There are several areas of which one can specialize in psychological science.

1) Clinical Psychology: Clinical psychologists assess and treat people with psychological problems. They many act as therapists for people experiencing normal psychological crises (e.g., grief) or for individuals suffering from chronic psychiatric disorders. Some clinical psychologists are generalists who work with a wide variety of populations, while others work with specific groups like children, the elderly, or those with specific disorders (e.g., schizophrenia). They may be found in hospitals, community health centers, private practice, or academic settings.

2) Counseling Psychology: Counseling psychologists do many of the same things that clinical psychologists do. However, counseling psychologists tend to focus more on persons with adjustment problems, rather than on persons suffer-

ing from severe psychological disorders. Counseling psychologists are employed in academic settings, community mental health centers, and private practice. Resent research tends to indicate that training in counseling and clinical psychology are very similar.

3) Developmental Psychology: Developmental psychologists study how we develop intellectually, socially, emotionally, and morally during our lifespan. Some focus on just one period of life (e.g., childhood or adolescence). Developmental psychologists usually do research and teach in academic settings, but many act as consultants to day-care centers, schools, or social service agencies.

4) Experimental Psychology: This area of specialization includes a diverse group of psychologists who do research in the most basic areas of psychology (e.g., learning, memory, attention, cognition, sensation, perception, motivation, and language). Sometimes their research is conducted with animals instead of humans. Most of these psychologists are faculty members at colleges and universities.

5) Educational Psychology: Educational psychologists are concerned with the study of human learning. They attempt to understand the basic aspects of learning and then develop materials and strategies for enhancing the learning process. For example, an educational psychologist might study reading and develop a new technique for teaching reading from the results of the research.

6) Social Psychology: Social psychologists study how our beliefs, feelings, and behaviors are affected by other persons. Some of the topics of interest to social psychologists are attitudes, aggression, prejudice, love, and interpersonal attraction. Most social psychologists are on the faculty of colleges and universities, but an increasing number are being hired by hospitals, federal agencies, and businesses to perform applied research.

7) School Psychology: School psychologists are involved in the development of children in educational settings. They are typically involved in the assessment of children and the recommendation of actions to facilitate students' learning. They often act as consultants to parents and administrators to optimize the learning environments of specific students.

8) Industrial/Organizational Psychology: Industrial/Organizational (I/O) psychologists are primarily concerned with the relationships between people and their work environments. They may develop new ways to increase productivity or be involved in personnel selection. You can find I/O psychologists in businesses, industry, government agencies, and colleges and universities. I/O psychologists are probably the most highly paid psychologists.

9) Physiological Psychology: Physiological psychology is one of psychology's hottest areas because of the recent dramatic increase in interest in the physiological correlates of behavior. These psychologists study both very basic processes

(e.g., how brain cells function) and more observable phenomena (e.g., behavior change as a function of drug use or the biological/genetic roots of psychiatric disorders). Some physiological psychologists continue their education in clinical areas and work with people who have neurological problems.

10) Environmental Psychology: Environmental psychologists are concerned with the relations between psychological processes and physical environments ranging from homes and offices to urban areas and regions. Environmental psychologists may do research on attitudes toward different environments, personal space, or the effects on productivity of different office designs.

11) Health Psychology: Health psychologists are concerned with psychology's contributions to the promotion and maintenance of good health and the prevention and treatment of illness. They may design and conduct programs to help individuals stop smoking, lose weight, manage stress, prevent cavities, or stay physically fit. They are employed in hospitals, medical schools, rehabilitation centers, public health agencies, and in private practice.

12) Family Psychology: Family psychologists are concerned with the prevention of family conflict, the treatment of marital and family problems, and the maintenance of normal family functioning. They design and conduct programs for marital enrichment, pre-marital preparation, and improved parent-child relations. They also conduct research on topics such as child abuse, family communications patterns, and the effects of divorce and remarriage. Family psychologists are often employed in medical schools, hospitals, community agencies, and in private practice.

13) Rehabilitation Psychology: Rehabilitation psychologists work with people who have suffered physical deprivation or loss at birth or during later development as a result of damage or deterioration of function (e.g., resulting from a stroke). They help people overcome both the psychological and situational barriers to effective functioning in the world. Rehabilitation psychologists work in hospitals, rehabilitation centers, medical schools, and in government rehabilitation agencies.

14) Psychometrics and Quantitative Psychology: Psychometric and quantitative psychologists are concerned with the methods and techniques used to acquire and apply psychological knowledge. A psychometrist reviews old intelligence, personality, and aptitude tests and devises new ones. Quantitative psychologists assist researchers in psychology or other fields to design experiments or interpret their results. Psyhchometrists and quantitative psychologists are often employed in colleges and universities, testing companies, private research firms, and government agencies.

15) Psychology and the Law and Forensic Psychology: Psychology and the law studies legal issues from a psychological perspective (e.g., how juries decide cases)

and psychological questions in a legal context (e.g., how jurors assign blame or responsibility for a crime). Forensic psychologists are concerned with the applied and clinical facets of the law such as determining a defendant's competence to stand trial or if an accident victim has suffered physical or neurological damage. Jobs in these areas are in law schools, research organizations, community mental health agencies, and correctional institutions.

Other areas of specialization include psychology and the arts, history of psychology, psychopharmacology, and community, comparative, consumer, engineering, population, and military.

Chapter 5

Insider's Advice on Graduate School Admissions Procedures

Insider's Advice on
Graduate School Admissions Procedures

Graduate school admission is a combination of how you look on paper and your connections in the field. That is why it is important that during your undergraduate years you cultivate positive relationships with your professors as well as with other individuals in the field. **Network, network, network.** Let those you work with know you are applying during the early phases of the process. For example, they may provide you with useful "inside" information about whom to direct your contacts to at a certain institution. You need to use your contacts wisely.

Building yourself into an attractive candidate begins the moment you declare psychology as your major. Ideally that would be in your freshman year, however, this is often not the case. Many individuals use their first year in college for exploration and discovery. That's ok, but the important thing is that once you have decided that psychology is the major for you, the preparation for graduate school admissions begins. There are many components that must be in place in order to increase your acceptance into a graduate program. Graduate admissions selection committees are comprised of the faculty at the program to which you apply. A survey of graduate institutions suggests that your GPA, Graduate Record Examination (GRE) scores, letters of recommendation, personal statement and research and clinical experience are all very important (Landrum, Jeglum, & Cashin, 1994). Unfortunately, student perception of the admission criteria may not be accurate. Nauta (2000) found that many undergraduates tended to underestimate the importance of letters of recommendation and overestimate minimum cutoff grade point averages. Hence, you need to understand that everything component of the application is important! Again, we cannot emphasize enough the importance of starting early in your undergraduate career to gain the experiences that will transform you into an attractive applicant. What follows is a guideline highlighting what you need to make yourself into an attractive candidate.

Psychology Courses and Recommended Plan

As a psychology major you already have a preference toward courses in this discipline. Within the major, there are courses that can develop a good foundation for future graduate training. Obviously, Introduction to Psychology (or General Psychology) is the foundation course for the major. It is typically the prerequisite for all other courses. This is a challenging course for most individuals as each chapter is in and of itself a course that can be taken later on. Think of the Introduction to Psychology course as a buffet table, where you can sample a wide variety of areas in this field. Reading your General Psychology textbook and having discussions with your advisor(s) and mentor(s) will provide you with information about course selection for the major and your specialized field of study (e.g., clinical, experimental, industrial/organizational).

There will most likely be a core set of courses you are required to take for the major. This varies from program to program. At one of the author's program, the core classes include General Psychology, Statistics, Physiological Psychology, Experimental Psychology, and Contemporary Issues in Psychology. In addition to the core classes, you can take a set number of electives in the psychology program. You will want to choose your electives wisely in order to develop a specialty track. For example, if a student aspires to work in the field of Clinical Psychology, taking Developmental Psychology courses, Abnormal Psychology, Psychological Testing, Physiological Psychology, and Introduction to Clinical Psychology are highly recommended. McGovern and Hawks (1986) stress the importance of taking a Careers in Psychology course to help broaden your knowledge of the field. Depending on the institution, there exists a tremendous amount of variance in the courses one can take.

It is interesting to note the many different ways there are to name a course. Nevertheless, you can see that these courses fall into general categories, for example, introduction to the field, human development, clinical/counseling skills, research skills and so on. With this wide variety it can be overwhelming to decide what you want to take. Meetings with your faculty advisor can be a chance to explore your thoughts and select courses that support your future plan.

In addition to the courses you must take for your major, you will be required to take General Education courses and other various electives. These courses provide additional opportunity for you to build your knowledge and round out your skills. From these additional courses, you can decide upon an advantageous minor or you may choose to double major. As an example, it can be helpful for individual who are interested in using their psychology training with delinquent minors or adult offenders to take courses in criminal justice—one may even chose a criminal justice minor or double major in psychology and criminal justice. One of our students, who was a double major in psychology and criminal justice, won admission to a forensic psychology doctoral program because of her unique combination of majors. If you are interested in industrial/organizational psychology, take courses in the business department. Nevertheless, the selection of courses for the Psychology major should follow a planful balance of core courses and electives within the major to expand your interest and graduation electives.

It can be difficult to keep track of all that you are doing during your undergraduate years. It is important that you keep an organized record of courses taken as well as courses you would like to take. Keeping track of your GPA is equally important.

We Asked and the Results Are In:
Student Testimonials and the Importance of Extracurricular Experiences

Let's face it. Getting into graduate programs is a competitive process. You are up against many other individuals with similar GPAs, GRE scores, and the like. Many programs receive hundreds of applications each year; yet only allow in a select few. Knowing that, it is to your advantage to make yourself stand apart from the crowd. Graduate school admission is a combination of how you look on paper and your connections in the field. It is through these connections that you will find employment opportunities as well as individuals who can write glowing letters of recommendation for graduate school. That is why it is important during your undergraduate years you cultivate positive relationships with your professors as well as with other individuals in the field. Network, network, network. Let those you work with know you are applying during the early phases of the process. They may provide you with useful "inside" information about to whom you should direct your contacts at a certain institution. You need to use your contacts wisely. Remember: Experience through both fieldwork and research will not only provide you with valuable opportunities for learning, but will also demonstrate your interest in and dedication to the field.

The authors of this book contacted the clinical training directors at universities in Illinois, Indiana, and Wisconsin and asked them about the importance of fieldwork and research experience in their applicants. The response was overwhelmingly in favor of such experiences. Although some programs do not directly require it, admissions committees see these experiences as beneficial and demonstrative to one's interest in the field. According to this sample, the clinical training directors feel their respective programs prefer applicants who are multi-dimensional and have experience applying knowledge to clinical practice. As research is an important part of graduate training, applicants who can readily assist with a research project are more attractive as well. The clinical training directors emphasized repeatedly that you want to make yourself stand out from other applicants. As a future applicant you would be wise to collect a similar sampling from schools you would like to attend, but the responses will most likely be the same as outlined here.

Despite the importance of such experiences, many students do not take advantage of these opportunities or are unaware such opportunities even exist in their program. What follows is a brief description of how these programs can work. Interested students should discuss these options with their course instructors, department chairs, and advisors to best maximize their experience while in attendance at their respective programs.

Service Learning, Field Work Placements/Internships & Volunteer Experiences. Many programs offer a variety of experiences where students can "get their feet wet." It is important that students "test their vocational goals in a realistic work environment" (Malin & Timmreck, 1979). First, some undergraduate courses may offer service-learning options. These opportunities provide a chance to assist with the needs of other and upon reflection, identify one's own learning. An enhanced perspective on a topic can be obtained from service learning. Such an option typically requires the student to assist with service provision at an off-site location on a time-limited basis. For example, a course in Child & Adolescent Development may provide an option where students can work in an after-school center delivering prevention curriculum (e.g., substance use, violence). An Industrial/Organizational Psychology course may provide an option where students can assist with job training and teaching interview skills to the homeless. In addition to the off-site work, students are often required to write a paper illustrating the connection between their experience and the course material. This is a valuable opportunity to demonstrate your ability to apply what you are learning in the classroom to real life. Some programs offer a service-learning course, which can also be a way to gain experience while applying credit hours towards graduation.

Second, Field Work Placements/Internships are an additional means of gaining experience. Typically, you will register for this type of experience for course credit, so, although you will not receive financial compensation, you will be able to apply the experience toward your graduation credits. You will work at a site with regular supervision providing services to select populations. In addition, a faculty mentor on campus will assist you with the completion of a final project designed to demonstrate the link between your educational experience and the field experience/internship.

Volunteer experiences can be a wonderful opportunity to gain experience outside of the classroom. Many organizations are eager to enlist the assistance of college students interested in volunteering at their sites. Although the experiences mean extra time from your week with no financial incentive, the experience gained will be an invaluable contribution to your resume, which is now becoming a curriculum vitae (explained later in this chapter).

Be selective when choosing your volunteer opportunity. Visit the site first and ask for a job description. Be sure you are receiving proper supervision and have an opportunity to meet with your supervisor on a regular basis to help you consolidate the experience. Seek the advice of your psychology faculty to best maximize your experience. An opportunity that best fits your interests and has you engaged in activities more directly related to the field will benefit you greatly. Although a volunteer experience will not apply toward graduation credits, it can offer flexibility in scheduling the other experiences cannot.

As an additional benefit, some students are successful in securing employment as a result of their participation in such programs. Some sites are willing to hire those students who successfully demonstrate their abilities. Other students have found employment at other settings because they now have some formal experience. In addition, such placements provide valuable opportunities for networking.

Research. Psychology is a science, and as such, research is an important aspect in the career of all psychologists. Whether or not active research participation is part of your career objectives, it is important to develop the skills necessary to critically evaluate research. Psychologists who do not conduct research as part of their daily job do rely on research for diagnostic work and treatment planning. To that end, one must be a good consumer of research and be able to read it objectively and critically. If you do plan on going to graduate school or having a career in an academic setting, research involvement is paramount. As a student you should capitalize on the potential for involvement in research efforts in your department. Working on a project with one of your professors can be an exhilarating experience. Yes, you can expect to work hard, but the pay-off has exponential benefits.

1). You can cultivate a relationship with you professor. This person may eventually become a mentor to you–guiding you toward career opportunities and providing you with glowing letters of recommendation.
2). You will sharpen your library skills. The library and the reference desk team are your best friends. You may be asked to find articles related to the project at hand. Therefore, you will become intimately familiar with such library search systems as PsychInfo and Medline.
3). You will learn the fundamentals of research (e.g., experimental design, statistical analysis) as applied to the project.
4). Putting in a good effort will most likely be rewarded with a place on the authorship line of the poster or manuscript that results. (Regarding conferences, there is no greater thrill than going to your first conference and looking up you name in the index of the program book.)
5). Should the project be presented at a conference, you will have the opportunity to attend and meet others with interests similar to yours. The networking opportunities at conferences are not to be underestimated.

Your role on the project will largely be up to the professor. You may help collect data. You may assist in the statistical analysis. Writing a portion of the final paper can also be offered to you. Should the project be presented as a poster at a conference, you may be asked to help design the poster on which it will be displayed. As stated above, you may have the opportunity to attend the conference where you can meet others and experience psychological research at its best. Obviously, the more skills you have coming into a project, the greater your immediate involvement. That is not to say, however, that you cannot participate if you have not yet done this type of work. This is the opportunity you need to learn and develop the research-skills that graduate programs prefer to see in their applicants. Do not be afraid to ask for more responsibility or for opportunities to learn more about the project. Showing interest highlights your motivation as a dedicated student. For a professor, there is no greater feeling than to share excitement about a research area with a student.

If you are interested in a particular area of psychology that is not being researched at your institution, you may want to explore opportunities elsewhere. Research opportunities are available though local organizations. You could become involved in a research program at such agencies as Easter Seals or United Way. If you are interested in a particular graduate school, you may want to hook up with a project at a school you are interested in applying to later. Not only does research involvement provide you with the experiences associated with learning how to conduct it, but also provides you with valuable networking opportunities. In summary, research skill development includes:

- Extending your classroom experience by working on a faculty members' research program in areas that match course content.
- Consulting with a faculty member about a paper you have written to determine if it is presentation or publication level.
- Consulting with a mentor about your interests to exchange ideas and perhaps work on a project.
- Attend department sponsored and college sponsored research presentations to explore what others are doing.
- Volunteer on a project.
- Practice search skills by using various library search engines to locate information.
- Read psychology journals.
- Attend local psychology conferences.

Club Participation. Many institutions provide students with additional means of gathering experience and discussing topics of interests. Participation as a member of a psychology club or a national honors society chapter (e.g., Psi Chi) can be another way of gaining experience. Some institutions require their student organizations to complete volunteer/service requirements. As such, you can gain valuable experience by participating in those activities. In addition, some clubs function as a "journal club" where members read current articles and discuss them at weekly meetings. Other clubs function as "research clubs" where the primary focus is the completion of a variety of research projects for possible presentation. Some clubs partner up with other clubs/organizations to share common interests and activities. For example, the psychology club and biology club may pool resources for a neuroanatomy demonstration at a local hospital.

Mentorship What is mentoring? Mentoring is a reciprocal process by which an experienced person can give knowledge and skills to a less experienced person. The less experienced person obtains the knowledge and skills; the experienced person gains the satisfaction of participating in the process. Mentoring relationships vary in their focus and usually have a set period of time although the demarcation points from the beginning and the end of the relationship are less clear. The psychology faculty at your institution are a valuable mentoring resource. Many faculty function in other capacities outside of the university and provide services to various populations (e.g., consultation, private practice). As such, you can learn much more from faculty than the course curriculum. Tap into their wealth of experiential knowledge. Research and field placement ideas often come from the relationships students develop with their faculty. In addition, the better a faculty member knows you, the better the letter of recommendation can be offered on your behalf. Therefore, it is to the student's benefit to cultivate a genuine and reciprocal relationship with his/her faculty.

Testimonials

"As an undergrad my grades were excellent, my GRE scores were good, and my letters of recommendation were fantastic, but I needed something that would make me stand out from all the other applicants whose grades were also excellent, GRE scores were good, and the letters of recommendation were fantastic. So when a fellow student told me one of our professors needed research help, I jumped at the chance. Throughout my undergrad career, I was always told the importance of extracurricular activities in the field of psychology. Helping a professor with research is an <u>excellent</u> extracurricular activity. Plus, by helping a professor and doing the extra work, we were able to present the project at a conference, where we learned we were the only undergraduates there who were co-authors on a project. My part in the presentation really helped me get into graduate school, because by working on the project, I was able to stand out from other applicants. For me, the research project I was helping on was not a field I was specifically interested in, but I learned a lot from the experience. I learned how to search for information, prepare research, and write an abstract. The experience went above and beyond any of my undergraduate coursework, and I know I can use what I learned when I work in my graduate program. I know that research projects as a grad student are one of those unspoken, but necessary objectives of your program. Being a part of a research project really is something everyone should consider if they plan to go to graduate school. If you're not lucky enough to present at a conference, the knowledge you will get from being part of the research will help as a graduate student. You get experience that you may not get before entering a program, where research projects are necessary."—**Alissa Fial, clinical psychology graduate student.**

"Looking back on my experience from Elmhurst College, I have many memories particularly as a psychology student. I was given many opportunities that other students in other majors were not exposed to or fellow psychology students did not take advantage of. I was fortunate and aware enough of the benefits that service-learning projects had for me as an individual and as a prospective graduate student. Service learning projects help volunteers decrease self-centeredness, increase self-esteem, and increase your motivation to help other people. Service learning projects benefit the volunteer and the recipient. While I attended Elmhurst College, I volunteered by services at Hancock Academy, Public Action to Deliver Shelter, Inc. (DuPage PADS), and Kenwood United Church of Christ Soup Kitchen. At Hancock Academy, I was a group facilitator for ninth grade students who were at risk for gang involvement. DuPage PADS was an experience to remember, as I made beds and food for homeless people. Finally, at the Kenwood Church, I prepared and distributed food for the needy. All of these opportunities increased my awareness of the community and increased my sense of social and personal responsibility. In addition, these experiences confirmed my decision to attend graduate school to continue my aspirations to help individuals."—**Rene E. Pichler, clinical psychology graduate student.**

"As an undergraduate, I always hear people say, "Experience is the key." I am constantly being told that the more research experience, volunteer work or job experience I have under my belt, the more I will stand out when it comes time to apply for graduate school. I never realized how right they were or how much fun it could be until my sophomore year. Through a psychology course, I got the opportunity to teach "Life Skills Training" to a group of fifth graders. It was a great experience and a helpful one at that. Because I had the training to teach "Life Skills Training," I was offered a job to be in charge of an after school program for at risk youth implementing that program. Through my job experience I learned many skills to deal with at risk youth. For example, I learned the importance of listening to them when they were troubled or upset. All they needed was someone to listen to the, be their friend, and give them advice. I also learned conflict resolution skills and how to apply them to the kids when they have problems with one another. But most importantly, I learned the significance of being a role mode to those kids. The power of knowing that I made a difference in someone's life is such a reward in itself. Through all of this I learned that it is important to get out there and get experience under your belt. I am now a junior undergrad and am looking into participating in another after school program closer to home. Being able to say that I did all of this will really help set me aside from other applicants when applying to graduate school. Not only is this helping me get into graduate school, but it was a great experience and I had a great time doing it."—**Nicole Kwasniewski, undergraduate psychology student.**

"**Get involved, gain research experience, present at student symposiums,**" words that have proved to be the very recipe that helped me to gain successful entrance into graduate school, and more importantly the program of choice. In fact, the day I realized I wanted to pursue an advanced degree in clinical psychology, I started asking faculty members and mentors for advice on how to make the transition from an undergraduate to "graduate student to be." To this day, I believe it was that advice that set the wheels in motion. First and foremost you do need to get involved. Involve yourself in any activity that is tied into your personal interests, whether it is helping others, working with children, or simply volunteering your time. Not only will the experience help you use the skills and information you learn in the classroom but it will make your overall educational experience more meaningful and significant. Secondly, gain as much research experience as you can. In other words, be proactive in approaching faculty members who share your interest and inquire about ways you can help them with their research. There are often many opportunities available to assist them in collecting and analyzing data, as well as helping with manuscript drafts, etc. This is a great way to demonstrate your critical thinking ability and your desire to pursue a graduate degree. Finally take pride in the work that you do and share it with others. You should make every attempt to present at, or attend, as many academic conferences as possible. Keep in mind that good grades and GRE scores can't hurt your changes of getting in, but they are not the "end all, be all." Identify your strengths and maximize your personal potential in a way that will make you an appealing applicant to any graduate program—**Amanda Urban, clinical psychology graduate student.**

"For two days each week for eight weeks one summer, I interned at Norwood Park Home, an assisted living facility, in Chicago, Illinois, and because of my interest and studies in adult development, I was assigned to the social services department. There I worked individually with the residents, providing a willing ear to listen to their concerns, overseeing their adjustment to new surroundings, and acting as an advocate for any problems or misunderstandings that occurred with the medical or administrative staff members, with other residents, or with family members.

"I delighted in helping the residents, and found the internship very informative. I had a great opportunity to work with the older adult on a daily basis, balancing what I had learned in the classroom with what I had discovered from practical application.

"As a direct result of observing the adjustment difficulties the residents faced, and after graduation, I created a serialized problem for encouraging the long-term facility resident to better adjust to the changes encountered. A pilot of the program was successfully facilitated, and future plans provide for the program to be made available to the general older adult population."

—**Nancy Stewart, undergraduate psychology student**

The Graduate Record Exam

The three most anxiety provoking words to most graduate school applicants are: Graduate Record Exam (GRE). When working with students, most faculty find that the GRE tends to be the topic that instills the most fear and anxiety. Even the calmest and most together students shutter at the mention of these words. Where does all this anxiety come from? Well, many students believe that this one set of scores will make or break their application. Some students have heard that graduate programs use these numbers as the initial cut-off for inviting applicants for interviews. Indeed that can be the case (Sternberg & Williams, 1997). Sadly, the use of these numbers as well as the fears students have are based in reality.

Many studies (e.g., House & Johnson, 2002; Chernyshenko & Ones, 1999; Symons, 1999) have supported the validity of the GRE with respect to graduate school success. Hence, virtually every graduate program in psychology requires the GRE. It consists of two separate three hour tests: (a) the General Text (composed of sections measuring verbal, quantitative, and analytical abilities) and (b) a Subject Test that measures understanding of basic psychological principles and facts. Some graduate programs require only the General Test, and the verbal and mathematical scores of the General Test are commonly viewed as most important. What tests are required will be in the information you obtained from the graduate program. You should obtain a copy of the GRE Information Bulletin (that contains an application form and sample test questions) from the appropriate academic office at your school. Be aware of registration deadlines and where the test will be offered.

You can prepare for the GRE, but it takes a commitment on your part. You will want to give yourself several months before the exam date to familiarize yourself with the test. Review classes (e.g., Kaplan) can be helpful. There are several published study guides for the GRE that you can purchase. These guides often contain older versions of the exams (with answers) for your use. Do not be discouraged if your first attempts are less successful than you had hoped. Repeatedly taking practice exams will increase your familiarity with the material and decrease your anxiety.

Again, it is important that you put a good effort into your preparation. Keep in mind that once you take it, your scores stay on record for five (5) years. If you do not do as well as you would have liked and you retake the exam, both sets of scores will be sent to the graduate programs. Some graduate programs will take the highest scores; some will average them, etc.

A closing comment on the GRE: As pointed out by Sternberg and Williams (1988), the GRE pulls for the emphasis that many colleges/universities place on "memory and analytical skills in (a) ability testing, (b) instruction, and (c) assessment." While the GRE can predict your memory and analytical skills, it does not pull for the creative and practical skills also necessary for success in graduate school. The other psychology experiences you have (e.g., field work, research opportunities, student projects) as well as the general education curriculum already discussed in this chapter help to round you out beyond what the GRE can measure. This is why you are represented by an application packet and not just a set of scores—so take a deep breath and relax.

How To Prepare A Personal Statement
Knowing What Makes You So Great!

Most graduate schools require a personal statement as a part of your application. This statement is often centered around your interest in psychology, your personal background, the reasons you are applying to that particular graduate program, and your career objectives. It is also a writing sample. Although a well-written personal statement will not overcome poor grades or low GRE scores, a poor one will surely hurt your changes of acceptance. Fretz and Stang (1998) cite the following example.

"Take the case of the student with a competitive grade point average and good references who was not accepted to any of the 11 programs he applied for. One cannot be sure, but the biographical statement included with his applications is the suspected reason. First, it was poorly typed, with many smears and crossed-out words. The spelling and grammar were both appalling. Finally, the content left much to be desired. It was far too long—about 15 pages—and went into detail about this person's philosophy of life (which was far from the establishment viewpoint). It also stressed emotional agonies and turning points in his life. Hoping to cure the world of all its evils, this person tried to indicate how a Ph.D. in psychology was necessary to fulfill that end. In short, it was an overstated, ill-conceived essay that may have been received so badly that it overshadowed his other attributes and data" (p.45).

Plan and produce your personal statement as carefully as you would a crucial term paper. The following tips (Fretz & Stang, 1988) will help you produce an impressive and effective personal statement.

1). Word-process your personal statement. It will require a series of drafts, and the inconvenience of rewriting each draft with a conventional typewriter can make you willing to settle for a less-than-perfect final product.

2). Before you begin your statement for each school, read as much about their program as possible so that you can tailor your statement to the program and convince the admissions committee that you will fit their program like a glove. "Each year many applicants will write, for example, that they want to attend the counseling psychology program at University X because they want to learn how to counsel emotionally handicapped children—even though the program specifies in its brochure that is does not provide training for work with young children. The selection committee immediately rejects those candidates."

3). Prepare an outline of the topics you want to cover (e.g., professional objectives and personal background) and list supporting material under each main topic. Write a rough draft in which you transform your outline into prose. Set it aside and read it a week later. If it still sounds good, go to the next stage. If not, rewrite it until it sounds right.

4). Check you spelling, grammar, punctuation, and capitalization carefully. Nothing detracts from the contents of a statement more than these types of errors. Avoid slang words that make you sound uneducated, and overly elaborate words of stilted language that will make you appear pompous or pretentious.

5). Ask two of your teachers to read your first rough draft and make suggestions. Incorporate these suggestions into your second rough draft. Ask for another reading and set of suggestions, and then prepare your final statement.

6). Your final statement should be as brief as possible—two double-spaced pages are sufficient. Stick to the points requested by each program, and avoid lengthy personal or philosophical discussions. If your statement sounds egocentric or boring, those who read it will assume you are egocentric or boring.

Do not feel bad if you do not have a great deal of experience in psychology to write about. Few individuals who are about to graduate from an undergraduate program do! Be sure to explain your relevant experiences (e.g., Service Learning or research projects), but do not try to turn them into events of cosmic proportion. Be honest, sincere, and objective—that is the only way to impress those evaluating your application.

Obtaining Letters of Recommendation for Graduate School
Know Who Your Friends Are

Whether you are applying for a job or admittance into a graduate program, you will be asked to provide references. These will usually be in the form of a letter of recommendation. Therefore, it is important to cultivate positive relationships with professors and employers from whom you wish to obtain this material. Graduate school applications will come with instructions and typically a form you will need to give your letter writer. When approaching an individual about writing a letter on your behalf, you needn't feel shy. Professors and employers alike anticipate doing this for their underlings. What you want to do is make the job easy for them. Provide them with a typed list of the names and addresses to whom the letters must be sent. If there are deadlines, provide those as well. Indicate which are sent directly to the institution, and which you will need to send with your completed packet. Make sure you have completed the demographic portion of the letter of recommendation forms. Also, it is critical that you indicate that you waive the right to see your letters of recommendation. Otherwise, admissions committees may feel that you have seen the letters thereby influencing what was written. Being straightforward and organized in your approach will insure the best and most favorable outcome.

Selection committees (as well as employers) take these recommendations very seriously. Therefore, the letter of recommendation should come from an individual who knows you well. You want to choose an individual who will write a glowing letter on your behalf. For example, let's say you have put in time volunteering your services to collect data for a psychology research project conducted by Dr. Mentor. You know from unsolicited feedback that you have been doing a good job. You have also had an opportunity to get to know Dr. Mentor, who is running the project, and have dazzled her with your knowledge about psychology. This person would obviously be a good choice for a letter of recommendation. You have not only worked for her, but she knows you as a hard-working, motivated, and dedicated individual. Another great letter may come from the supervisor you have been working under as a Psychology Tech for the last two years at a local retirement center. Letters can come from your superiors in a volunteer setting as well.

Getting the Information

Now that you have prepared yourself with the experiences described earlier in this chapter, it is time to explore where you want to go. Applications for graduate school (especially at the doctoral level) are generally due around the same time every year. Most programs do not practice rolling admissions (i.e., accepting applications year round), and have their application deadlines sometime in December. Be sure to be cognizant of all deadlines for applications. When looking for programs, one of the first places to start is in any of the resource books that offer descriptions of graduate programs in psychology (e.g., Peterson's Graduate and Professional Programs, 2000). These books contain, by discipline and in alphabetical order, complete listings of every graduate program in the country. From there, you can obtain names and addresses. After discovering what institutions are out there, you should visit each website to preview the program. A comparison of curriculum and opportunities can help you decide where to spend your mental energy and money for application fees. Next you will want to contact the institutions of interest and request the following information:

1). Specific information concerning your clinical program. (e.g., faculty, special opportunities, and requirements for admission)
2). The theoretical orientation of the program.
3). Information about the availability and cost of graduate student housing.
4). Financial aid information, including teaching assistantships, research assistantships, etc.
5). A graduate catalog from the institution.
6). An application for admission into your clinical psychology program

Closing Pieces of Advice on Admissions: Know What You're Getting Into

Obviously the process of preparing for graduate school cannot happen over night. Students who want to go directly from undergraduate to graduate training must start the process early in their education. If that is the case, you should spend your Junior year gathering research and field experience, as well as prepare for the GRE. Your Senior year is spent completing additional field experience, concluding (and hopefully presenting) your research involvement, and preparing your applications. Again, watch those deadlines! This can be a tall order when you are in the midst of writing papers and studying for exams in your current classes. Good time management and organizational skills will make this an easier process. Obviously, you will have to expend some effort to increase the chances of your acceptance into a graduate program. It is easy to become overwhelmed and intimidated by the process. Understandably, you may feel as though you are under a microscope. Do not forget that you are also evaluating the program's fit for your needs, just as they are evaluating you as a fit for their needs. With that in mind, you will want to further your research of graduate programs to include issues such issues as lifestyle and time to completion. As mentioned in this book, there are several alternative graduate degrees in psychology for you to choose from. Each varies in terms of application procedures, admission criteria, academic curriculum, and prospective employment alternatives. It is important to research these areas thoroughly so as to make an informed decision regarding your academic aspirations.

<u>Now What?</u>
<u>Once Your Application is In</u>

Once received, the institution will plow through all applications and select several outstanding candidates for interviews. Do your homework before the interview. If possible, find out with whom you will be interviewing and become familiar with his/her most recent research. A PsychInfo search can be quite illuminating. Conduct a practice interview with one of your professors. The practice interview also gives you a chance to see if you feel comfortable in this situation. After the interview, send thank you letters to those with whom you interviewed.

Do not get discouraged should you not gain admittance on the first try. According to a recent survey, acceptance rates of clinical and counseling PhD programs were between 6-8% (Norcross, Sayette, Mayne, Karg, & Turkson, 1988). Graduate school is competitive, but there are strategies you can use to enhance your changes the second time around. Use that year between application deadlines to your advantage and beef up your resume/curriculum vitae, or network, network, network. You may want to get involved in research at a particular graduate institution. Speak with your undergraduate professors about additional research opportunities. Attend classes at your institution of choice as a student at large and get to know the faculty. Gain additional experience through employment or volunteer opportunities. Showing that you are a serious and dedicated student is just as important as your GPA and GRE scores.

Major Entry #5

Go onto the Web and locate five graduate programs in your state and three out-of-state programs.

1. *List faculty that you can contact about field and research opportunities.*

2. *List the courses required to earn the degree.*

3. *Look at the entrance requirements and list criteria that you can meet or exceed.*

4. *Construct a text table with this information. Include university contact information such as person's name, address, phone number, fax number, and email.*

Chapter 6

Degrees, Training, Earnings, and Employment

Major Entry #6

Consult your local paper to generate a list of 10-15 viable employment opportunities that you would like to do. Modify the list to reflect positions you are eligible to enter now and those that you need training for.

Set up informational interviews with professionals in mental health (e.g., MA Clinical Psychology, PhD/PsyD) and find out what types of job opportunities they have available to them with that degree.

DEGREES AND TRAINING

Don't be scared away by this title! As you have selected the Psychology major and are carving a path to complete the degree you will soon experience these outcomes. Obtaining your degree and additional training needs to be planned. An objective, once identified, of what you would like to do can be realized with a good plan.

This chapter lays out the basic information that you need for this plan. Hopefully, your "Major Entry #3" provided you with a sufficient opportunity to identify your objectives.

Baccalaureate Degree. While the baccalaureate degree is somewhat limited in terms of positions in mental health, there are a variety of options that do not require a license to practice. (Licensure is explained below.) This degree qualifies a person to assist psychologists and other professionals in community mental health centers, vocational rehabilitation offices, and correctional programs; to work as research or administrative assistants; to function as psychometrists, program coordinators, program directors; to serve as grant writers; or work as trainees in government or business. However, without additional academic training, their advancement opportunities in psychology are severely limited. An article by Murray (2002) offers helpful suggestions for those looking for employment with baccalaureate degrees in psychology.

Master's Degree. Persons with a master's degree in psychology can conduct research in laboratories, conduct psychological evaluations, perform administrative duties, work in training and organizational development departments, or work in human resources departments. Many states offer licensure at this level, where by one can work as a therapist in independent practice. Graduates with a master's degree in psychology may encounter competition for the limited number of jobs for which they qualify, but those with the license at the master's level will do better in the job market. Many work as clinicians in private practice and hospital settings. Having licensure increases your marketability because you can be recognized by insurance companies as a service provider, and do not necessarily require supervision for psychotherapy services.

A master's degree program will take approximately 2-3 years to complete. Requirements generally include your coursework and a master's thesis and/or field placement. One piece of advise—if you are planning on eventually attending a doctoral program, you are best advised to do the master's thesis rather than the field placement if given the option to complete only one or the other. The reason being that since one can enter a PhD/PsyD program with a baccalaureate degree, you will have to transfer your master's degree into the doctoral program and hope you will get credit for your efforts. The more that transfers in, the fewer courses you will have to repeat. Most doctoral programs will accept your thesis, but not the field placement.

Doctoral Degree. A doctoral degree is necessary for employment as a psychologist. Psychologists with this advanced training qualify for a wide range of teaching, research, clinical, and counseling positions in universities, elementary and secondary schools, private industry, and government.

Clinical Psychology Doctoral Programs: Ph.D., PsyD., and Lifestyle

There are several things to consider when applying to doctoral programs in clinical psychology. For both Ph.D. and Psy.D. programs, you want to attend a school that "jives" with your theoretical belief system. Each individual graduate program will "specialize" in a particular psychological orientation. For example, one program may be Psychodynamic, while another embraces Cognitive-Behavioral theoretical perspectives. If you are oriented toward Psychodynamic theory, you will be unhappy in a Cognitive-Behavioral program.

For Ph.D. programs, you will not only be admitted into the program as a whole, but you are also admitted into a lab, under your advisor, where you will be expected to work on research. Within the graduate program at a particular institution, each faculty member runs a lab that specializes in different areas of research. For example, within one school there may be five faculty with five respective labs. One lab may be conducting research in the area of sports psychology, another in behavioral medicine, another in crisis intervention. When selecting a program, the "best fit" not only comes from the theoretical orientation, but also from your research interests. Faculty will look through your application to see how good a fit you are to the research focus of their respective labs. This is why you should spend time researching the research focus of the faculty at the institutions to which you wish to apply.

As mentioned, clinical psychology programs come in two different models of training. Ph.D. programs are designed from a Scientist-Practitioner Model and Psy.D. programs from a Practitioner Model. Those who offer a Ph.D. and those that offer a Psy.D. (Regardless, it is best to choose a program that is approved by the American Psychological Association—not all are). While both will earn you the title "doctor" they offer somewhat different educational and occupational experiences. You need to decide which is best for you. There are several factors to consider. Ph.D. programs generally admit fewer students per year than Psy.D. programs. For example, a Ph.D. program may admit 10 students where as a Psy.D. program may admit 50 students. As Psy.D. programs are more clinically oriented, a Psy.D. program may not be as interested in research work as a Ph.D.

program. In terms of curriculum, Psy.D. and Ph.D. programs which are accredited by the American Psychological Association must offer similar core classes. There may be differences, however in other course offerings and the emphasis placed on them. For example, Ph.D. programs require more statistical and research coursework than Psy.D. programs.

An additional difference between the two programs is lifestyle. In general, Ph.D. programs follow a fairly traditional scheduling of courses. Courses usually meet once per week for three hours. You will generally be expected to be a full-time student for the first portion of your academic career. In addition to your coursework, you will be required to participate in research projects related to your lab. Psy.D. programs do not have the same research/lab requirements. In addition, many programs offer classes through non-traditional scheduling. For example, some programs offer classes that offer once a month on Saturday with assignments in between meeting times. Unsolicited commentary from Psy.D students would appear to reflect a lifestyle more conducive to an individual who must continue to hold employment throughout graduate school.

In addition to your coursework (and lab responsibilities if you are in a Ph.D. program), you will be expected to complete practicum/externship placements. These are placements, typically 20 hours per week, where you will gain direct field experience in clinical psychology—both diagnostic and therapeutic work. The process for gaining a practicum placement is well organized through your school. Your job is to decide what type of experience you would like and who offers the best training in that area. For example, you want to gain experience in psychological assessment with the pediatric population. Therefore, you should discuss your desire with the practicum coordinator who can suggest sites specific to your goals. Practicum placements may be offered at various hospitals, residential facilities, large group practices, etc. In addition, you will be working on a Master's thesis–an original research project–with your faculty advisor.

Both Ph.D. and Psy.D. programs will require you to pass a comprehensive examination. These vary from institution to institution and can take various forms:

➢ oral (committee of your choice)
➢ oral (committee chosen for you)
➢ written (on site)
➢ written (take home)
➢ oral and written (with various combinations regarding type)

Don't panic. Your institution will provide you with the skills necessary to successfully complete this requirement. Do take it seriously. Some students pass on the first try; others pass, but must make revisions; others fail. Should you fail to pass it as per the institutional guidelines, you will lose your place in the program.

The Ph.D. degree will require a dissertation based on original research. The Psy.D degree requires, for example, a clinical research project, which is more flexible in its design (e.g., extended case study). Regardless, this project represents the culmination of your academic experience. It is your project from start to finish (with the guidance of your advisor), that must be defended in front of and passed by a committee of your faculty members.

Lastly, both programs will require you to complete a clinical internship. Traditionally, internships last for one year and represent last pre-doctoral training experience. It is a nationally coordinated event where all doctoral candidates apply for pre-doctoral positions at internship sites through a very specific and regimented process. Internship applications, much like graduate school applications, are due once a year. Typically, they are due in late November/early December. It is best to choose an internship that is approved by the American Psychological Association. Once your applications have been reviewed, you may be asked to interview at certain sites. The notification of your acceptance into an internship site is completed through a nationally coordinated system that occurs on-line during a specified date in February. On that day, you will find out where you have been placed, and huge amounts of relief will set in. This is a stressful period, since there are often more applicants than placements. Some individuals will not be placed the first time (for various reasons) and will have to try again the following year. Keep in mind, the above narrative is a very brief run through of internship procedures. Your graduate program will provide you with the assistance you need to be successful in this venture. What's important to recognize is that this is the last of your formalized training under the pre-doctoral level–make the most of it. As you can see, it can take between 5 to 7 years to complete a doctoral degree. This may seem like a long time, but you are entering a field where you have an enormous influence in people's lives. You better know what you're doing!

Certification & Licensure

Psychologists in independent practice or those who offer any type of patient care, including clinical, counseling, and school psychologists, must meet certification or licensing requirements. All states and the District of Columbia have such requirements. Licensing laws vary by state, but generally require a doctorate in psychology, completion of an approved internship, and 1 to 2 years of professional experience. In addition, most states require that applicants pass an examination. Most state boards administer a standardized test, and, in many instances, additional oral or essay examinations. Several states have enacted requirements allowing licensure with a master's degree in psychology (mentioned above). Some states require continuing education for license renewal. Most states require that licensed or certified psychologists limit their practice to those areas in which they have developed professional competence through training and experience.

Beyond the license, advanced credentialing is also available. This is similar to the physician's ability to become board certified in a specific area of practice. You may have noticed on your physician's business cards additional letters following the M.D. at the end of their name (e.g., FAAP, Fellow of the American Academy of Pediatrics). Psychologists have similar opportunities, which are offered through various credentialing entities. The American Board of Professional Psychology (ABPP) is the largest credentialing group and recognizes professional achievement by awarding diplomas primarily in clinical, clinical neuropsychology, counseling, forensic, industrial/organizational, and school psychology. Candidates need a doctorate in psychology, a specified number of years of experience, and professional endorsements in order to apply. Once deemed eligible, they must pass a series of exams before the diploma is awarded.

Earnings

According to a 1999 survey by the American Psychological Association (Williams, Wicherski, &. Kohout, 2000), salaries vary tremendously depending upon the setting in which one works, licensure status, specialty area of practice, and so on. The survey data is available on-line at the following website address: http://research.apa.org/99salaries.html. As an example of what is available at this website, the following is offered. Licensed individuals who have been working in private practice for 2-4 years have an average salary of $43,556, as compared to those practicing from 5-9 years who have an average salary of $67,667. For those interested in pursuing a career in Industrial/Organizational psychology, the average salary for an individual employed in a consulting firm for 2-4 years is $59,111. If you continue in that career for another 5-9 years, the average salary is $101,222. The wealth of information at this website cannot possible be represented thoroughly here, so readers are strongly encouraged to access this website to get the best idea of what the salaries in this field are like.

Working Conditions for Psychologists

A psychologist's specialty and place of employment determine working conditions. For example, psychologists in private practice have their own offices and set their own hours. Although they often have evening hours to accommodate their clients, they have flexibility in scheduling their own hours of operation. Some employed in hospitals, nursing homes, and other health facilities often work evenings and weekends, while others in schools and clinics work regular hours. Psychologists employed by academic institutions divide their time among teaching, research, and administrative responsibilities. Some maintain part-time consulting practices as well. In contrast to the many psychologists who have flexible work schedules, most in government, hospital, and private industry have more structured schedules. Regardless, many psychologists travel to attend conferences and/or conduct research. For more detailed information on employment and work conditions, readers are encouraged to visit the APA website (www.apa.org). At the search window, enter salaries, and you will be rewarded with an extensive listing of links to information about these and related topics.

What the Future Holds

Employment of psychologists is expected to grow much faster than the average for all occupations through the year 2005. Largely because of the substantial investment in training required to enter this specialized field, psychologists have a strong attachment to their occupation; only a relatively small proportion leave the profession each year. Nevertheless, replacement needs are expected to account for most job openings, similar to most occupations.

Programs to combat the increase in alcohol abuse, drug dependency, marital strife, family-violent crime, and other problems plaguing society should stimulate employment growth. Other factors spurring demand for psychologists include increased emphasis on mental health maintenance in conjunction with the treatment of physical illness; public concern for the development of human resources, including the growing elderly population; increased testing and counseling of children; and more interest in rehabilitation of prisoners. Changes in the level of government funding for these kinds of services could affect the demand for psychologists.

Job opportunities in health care should remain strong, particularly in health care provided networks, such as health maintenance and preferred provider organizations, that specialize in mental health, and in nursing homes and alcohol and drug abuse rehabilitation programs. Job opportunities will arise in businesses, nonprofit organizations, and research and computer firms. Companies will use psychologists' expertise in survey design, analysis, and research to provide personnel testing, program evaluation, and statistical analysis. The increase in employee assistance programs, in which psychologists help people stop smoking, control weight, or alter other behaviors, also should spur job growth. The expected wave of retirement among college faculty, beginning in the late 1990's should result in job openings for psychologists in colleges and universities.

Other openings are likely to occur as psychologists study the effectiveness of changes in health, education, military, law enforcement, and consumer protection programs. Psychologists are also increasingly studying the effects on people of technological advances in areas such as agriculture, energy, the conservation and use of natural resources, and the industrial and office automation.

Chapter 7

Ethical Guidelines and Academic Honesty

Ethical Guidelines and Academic Honesty

Since its inception in 1992, the Ethics Code for Psychologists has stood as a set of standards for just professional behavior. As a major in Psychology you are a part of these requirements when your faculty member sponsors your research and supervises your fieldwork. As you enter the field you will be aware of the application of Ethics that you learned in such courses as Introductory Psychology, Abnormal Psychology, Child Psychology, and Research Methods. Hopefully, each of your Psychology courses addressed relevant ethical conduct.

In general, you should become aware of the ethical guidelines that psychologists follow as part of your undergraduate education. Some guidelines will be discussed with great detail in your research-based class (e.g., Research Methods, Experimental Psychology), where you will become familiar with such concepts as confidentiality and consent. Knowledge of ethical principles becomes especially critical when you decide to complete a field/training experience or work with a faculty member on a more extensive research project. To that end, the authors have reproduced, for your convenience, some general information regarding the American Psychological Association's Ethical Principles. These can be found in Appendix I. Whenever in doubt, you should discuss any and all ethical questions with faculty at your institution.

In addition, it is important that you observe the policies of academic honesty when completing your coursework. Plagiarism is one of the most unfortunate problems with which faculty must face in student work. Whether purposeful or accidental, it can result in failure of a project or the entire course. To that end, it is important to familiarize yourself with the APA Style Manual (2002). This source provides you with information regarding citing and referencing the original sources you may use for a written assignment. Information on how to use quotes and the like is also provided for your use. Many psychology instructors will require papers to be in APA format. This means following the guidelines set forth in the APA Style Manual. Your campus library should have copies available for your reference.

Characteristics of Ethical Dilemmas
- Ethical dilemmas are emotionally traumatic, no matter what your role in them.
- Ethical dilemmas are more likely in turbulent environments with rapidly changing norms.
- Ethical dilemmas frequently overlap with university politics and the law.
- In the peer-controlled environment of academics, most ethical dilemmas are also political.
- Ethical dilemmas are exacerbated by political fighting.
- Administrative procedures for dealing with ethical dilemmas may be weak or poorly defined.
- Administrative remedies for ethical dilemmas are only as good as the people who implement them.
- The impact of your strategy to deal with wrongdoing may depend on your professional power rather than on how right you are.
- The ultimate club in an ethical dilemma is the law and the pursuit of legal remedies.
- University administrators are often more concerned with minimizing conflict, establishing a smooth-functioning process, and avoiding lawsuits than with the outcome of any particular ethics violation case.

PREAMBLE TO
ETHICAL PRINCIPLES OF A PSYCHOLOGIST

Psychologists have an ethical code (Ethical Principles of Psychologists, APA, 1992) and a book for the interpretation and application of the code in specific situations (Casebook of Ethical Principles of Psychologists, APA, 1974). This code specifies the manner in which scientific research is conducted and services to clients are rendered. The preamble to this code is presented below to familiarize students with the nature of this publication.

Psychologists work to develop a valid and reliable body of scientific knowledge based on research. They may apply that knowledge to human behavior in a variety of contexts. In doing so, they perform many roles, such as researcher, educator, diagnostician, therapist, supervisor, consultant, administrator, social interventionist, and expert witness. Their goal is to broaden knowledge of behavior and, where appropriate, to apply it pragmatically to improve the condition of both the individual and society. Psychologists respect the central importance of freedom of inquiry and expression in research, teaching, and publication. They also strive to help the public in developing informed judgments and choices concerning human behavior. This Ethics Code provides a common set of values upon which psychologists build their professional and scientific work.

This code is intended to provide both the general principles and decision rules to cover most situations encountered by psychologists. It has as its primary goal the welfare and protection of the individuals and groups with whom psychologists work. It is the individual responsibility of each psychologist to aspire to the highest possible standards of conduct. Psychologists respect and protect human and civil rights, and do not knowingly participate in or condone unfair discriminatory practices.

The development of a dynamic set of ethical standards for psychologist's work-related conduct requires a personal commitment to a life-long effort to act ethically; to encourage ethical behavior by students, supervisees, employees, and colleagues, as appropriate; and to consult with others, as needed, concerning ethical problems. Each psychologist supplements, but does not violate, the Ethics Code's values and rules on the basis of guidance drawn from personal values, culture, and experience.

THE SIX GUIDING ETHICAL PRINCIPLES OF PSYCHOLOGISTS

The following principles are quoted directly from Ethical Principles of Psychologists (APA, 1992)

PRINCIPLE A: COMPETENCE

Psychologists strive to maintain high standards of competence in their work. They recognize the boundaries of their particular competencies and the limitations of their expertise. They provide only those services and use only techniques for which they are qualified by education, training, or experience. Psychologists are cognizant of the fact that the competencies required in serving, teaching, and/or studying groups of people vary with the distinctive characteristics of those groups. In those areas in which recognized professional standards do not yet exist, psychologists exercise careful judgment and take appropriate precautions to protect the welfare of those with whom they work. The maintain knowledge of relevant scientific and professional information related to the services they render, and they recognize the need for ongoing education. Psychologists make appropriate use of scientific, professional, technical, and administrative resources.

PRINCIPLE B: INTEGRITY

Psychologists seek to promote integrity in the science, teaching, and practice of psychology. In these activities, psychologists are honest, fair, and respectful of others. In describing or reporting their qualification, services, products, fees, research, or teaching, they do not make statements that are false, misleading, or deceptive. Psychologists strive to be aware of their own belief systems, values, needs, and limitations and the effect of these on their work. To the extent feasible, they attempt to clarify for relevant parties the roles they are performing and to function appropriately in accordance with those roles. Psychologists avoid improper and potentially harmful dual relationships.

PRINCIPLE C: PROFESSIONAL AND SCIENTIFIC RESPONSIBILITY

Psychologists uphold professional standards of conduct, clarify their professional roles and obligations, accept appropriate responsibility for their behavior, and adapt their methods to the needs of different populations. Psychologists consult with, refer to, or cooperate with other professionals and institutions to the extent needed to serve the best interest of their patients, clients, or other recipients of their service. Psychologists' moral standards and conduct are personal matters to the same degree as is true for any other person, except as psychologists' conduct may compromise their professional responsibilities or reduce the public's trust in psychology and psychologists. Psychologists are concerned about the ethical compliance of their colleagues' scientific and professional conduct. When appropriate, they consult with colleagues in order to prevent or avoid unethical conduct.

PRINCIPLE D: RESPECT FOR PEOPLE'S RIGHTS AND DIGNITY

Psychologists accord appropriate respect to the fundamental rights, dignity, and worth of all people. They respect the rights of individuals to privacy, confidentiality, self-determination, and autonomy, mindful that legal and other obligations may lead to inconsistency and conflict with the exercise of these rights. Psychologists are aware of cultural, individual, and role differences, including those due to age, gender, race, ethnicity, national origin, religion, sexual orientation, disability, language, and socioeconomic status. Psychologists try to eliminate the effect on their work of biases based on those factors, and they do not knowingly participate in or condone unfair discriminatory practice.

ETHICAL PRINCIPLES IN THE CONDUCT OF RESEARCH WITH HUMAN PARTICIPANTS

The following general principle and its ten sub-principles are quoted directly from Ethical Principles in the Conduct of Research with Human Subjects (APA, 1982, p. 5-7). Copies of this publication are available in the psychology office and the college library.

GENERAL PRINCIPLE:

The decision to undertake research rests upon a considered judgment by the individual psychologists about how best to contribute to psychological science and human welfare. Having made the decision to conduct research, the psychologists considers alternative directions in which research energies and resources might be invested. On the basis of this consideration, the psychologist carries out the investigation with respect and concern for the dignity and welfare of the people who participate and with cognizance of federal and state regulations and professional standards governing the conduct of research with human participants.

- In planning a study, the investigator has the responsibility to make careful evaluation of its ethical acceptability. To the extend that the weighing of scientific and human values suggests a compromise of any principle, the investigator incurs a correspondingly serious obligation to seek ethical advice and to observe stringent safeguards to protect the rights of human participants.
- Considering whether a participant in a planned study will be a "subject at risk" or a "subject at minimal risk," according to recognized standards, is of primary ethical concern to the investigator.
- The investigator always retains the responsibility for ensuring ethical practice in research. The investigator is also responsible for the ethical treatment of research participants by collaborators, assistants, students, and employees, all of whom, however, incur similar obligations.
- Except in minimal-risk research, the investigator establishes a clear and fair agreement with research participants, prior to their participation, that clarifies the obligation and responsibilities of each. The investigator has the obligation to honor all promises and commitments included in that agreement. The investigator informs all participants of all aspects of the research that might reasonably be expected to influence willingness to participate and explains all other aspects of the research about which the participant inquires. Failure to make full disclo-

sure prior to obtaining informed consent requires additional safeguards to protect the welfare and dignity of the research participants. Research with children or with participants who have impairments that would limit understanding and/or communication requires special safeguarding procedures.

• Methodological requirements of a study may make the use of concealment or deception necessary. Before conducting such a study, the investigator has a special responsibility to (a) determine whether the use of such techniques are justified by the study's prospective scientific, educational, or applied value; (b) determine whether alternative procedures are available that do not use concealment or deception; and (c) ensure that the participants are provided with sufficient explanation as soon as possible.

• The investigator respects the individual's freedom to decline to participate in or to withdraw from the research at any time. The obligation to protect this freedom requires careful thought and consideration when the investigator is in a position of authority or influence over the participant. Such positions of authority include, but are not limited to, situations in which research participation is required as part of employment or in which the participant is a student, client, or employee of the investigator.

• The investigator protects the participants from physical and mental discomfort, harm, and danger that may arise from research procedures. If risks of such consequence exist, the investigator informs the participant to that fact. Research procedures likely to cause serious or lasting harm to a participant are not used unless the failure to use these procedures might expose the participant to risk of greater harm, or unless the research has great potential benefit and fully informed and voluntary consent is obtained from each participant. The participant should be informed of procedures for contacting the investigator within a reasonable time period following participation should stress, potential harm, or related questions or concerns arise.

• After the data are collected, the investigator provides the participants with information about the nature of the study and attempts to remove any misconceptions that may have arisen. Where scientific or humane values justify delaying or withholding this information, the investigator incurs a special responsibility to monitor the research and to ensure that there are no damaging consequences for the participant.

• Where research procedures result in undesirable consequences for the individual participant, the investigator has the responsibility to detect and remove or correct these consequences, including long-term effects.

• Information obtained about a research participant during the course of an investigation is confidential unless otherwise agreed upon in advance. When the possibility exists that others may obtain access to such information, this possibility, together with the plans for protecting confidentiality, is explained to the participant as part of the procedures for obtaining informed consent.

THE RIGHTS AND RESPONSIBILITIES OF RESEARCH PARTICIPANTS

Students performing psychological research have an ethical obligation to (a) respect the rights of their research participants (e.g., subjects) and to (b) communicate their responsibilities to them. The following outline (taken directly from Korn, 1989) describes these rights and responsibilities of research participants.

A. The Rights of Research Participants

1. Participants should know the general purpose of the study and what they will be expected to do. Beyond this, they should be told everything a reasonable person would want to know in order to decide whether to participate.
2. Participants have the right to withdraw from a study at any time after beginning participation in the research. A participant who chooses to withdraw has the right to receive whatever benefits promised.
3. Participants should expect to receive benefits that out weight the costs or risks involved. To achieve the educational benefit, participants have the right to ask questions and receive clear, honest answers. When participants do not receive what was promised, they have the right to remove their data from the study.
4. Participants have the right to expect that anything done or said during their participation in a study will remain anonymous and confidential, unless they specifically agree to give up this right.
5. Participants have the right to decline to participate in any study and may not be coerced into research. When learning about research is a course requirement, an equivalent alternative to participation should be available.
6. Participants have the right to know when they have been deceived in a study and why the deception was used. If the deception seems unreasonable, participants have the right to withhold their data.
7. When any of these rights are violated or participants object to anything about a study, they have the right and responsibility to inform the appropriate university officials, including the chairperson of the psychology department.

B. The Responsibilities of Research Participants

1. Participants have the responsibility to listen carefully to the experimenter and ask questions in order to understand the research.

2. Be on time for the research appointment.
3. Participants should take the research seriously and cooperate with the experimenter.
4. When the study has been completed, participants share the responsibility of understanding what happened.
5. Participants have the responsibility for honoring the researcher's request that they do not discuss the study with anyone else who might be a participant.

THE CARE AND USE OF ANIMALS IN RESEARCH

The Principle E from <u>Ethical Principles of Psychologists</u> APA, 1992) deals with the care and use of animals in research.

GENERAL PRINCIPLE:

An investigator of animal behavior strives to advance understanding of basic behavioral principles and/or to contribute to the improvement of human health and welfare. In seeking these ends, the investigator ensures the welfare of animals and treats them humanely. Laws and regulations notwithstanding, an animal's immediate protection depends upon the scientist's own conscience.

- The acquisition, care, use, and disposal of all animals are in compliance with current federal, state or provincial, and local laws and regulations.
- A psychologist trained in research methods and experienced in the care of laboratory animals closely supervises all procedures involving animals and is responsible for ensuring appropriate considerations of their comfort, health, and humane treatment.
- Psychologists ensure that all individuals using animals under their supervision receive explicit instruction in experimental methods and in the care, maintenance, and handling of the species used. Responsibilities and activities of individuals participating in a research project are consistent with their competencies.
- Psychologists make every effort to minimize discomfort, illness, and pain of animals. A procedure subjecting animals to pain, stress, or deprivation is used only when an alternative procedure is unavailable and the goal is justified by its prospective scientific, educational, or applied value. Surgical procedures are performed under appropriate anesthesia; techniques to avoid infection and minimize pain are followed during and after surgery.
- When it is appropriate that the animal's life be terminated, it is done rapidly and painlessly.

Major Entry #7

Contact the student government and/or the Dean of Students at your institution to find out about an ethics committee at your school It is likely that there will be varied types such as a Research Review Board, Appeals Committee for Student Unethical Behavior, or Personnel Board for Faculty. Some institutions have these materials printed in Student Handbooks.

Locate the source as indicated above and attend one meeting.

ADDITIONAL RESOURCES

A Survival Guide
A resource for minority and women faculty members in academic institutions. Available from the Public Interest Directorate, 750 First St., NE, Washington, DC 20002-4242.

Psychology Education and Careers Guidebooks
A series of guidebooks for High School Students of Color; College Students of Color; College Students of Color Applying to Graduate and Professional Programs; and Psychology Training Programs Recruiting Students of Color. Available from the Public Interest Directorate, 750 First St., NE, Washington, DC 20002-4242

Ethnic Minority Job Bank Service
For ethnic minority psychologists seeking employment and also for employers seeking applicants. Contact the Office of Ethnic Minority Affairs, (202) 336-6029; 750 First St., NE, Washington, DC 20002-4242. Email: oema@apa.org.

American Psychological Association
www.apa.org

American Psychological Society
www.aps.org

Demonstrations, Tutorials, & Class Materials
http://www.uni.edu/walsh/tutor.html
This site is maintained by Dr. Linda Walsh from the University of Northern Iowa. The site contains numerous links to web sites of interest for faculty and introductory psychology students.

Classics in the History of Psychology
http://www.yorku.ca/dept/psych/classics/index.htm

This York University site provides access to pages devoted to classic articles and books on psychology topics. Among the authors covered are Plate, Skinner, James, Wundt, and Watson.

Today in the History of Psychology
http://www.cwu.edu/%7Ewarren/today.html
This site provides access to over 3100 critical or key events in the history of psychology. The site is organized by date and allows a person to determine the events that occurred on that date in the history of psychology.

Graduate School and Careers in Psychology
http://www.rider.edu/users/suler/gradschl.html
This site contains information on the various careers in psychology and information on graduate training in psychology.

The Psychology Hall of Fame
http://www.angelfire.com/tx/jcr/Psychology.html
This comprehensive web site provides students with access to short biographies of famous psychologists.

The University of Toronto Museum of Psychological Instruments
http://psych.utoronto.ca/museum/
One of the features that differentiated psychology as a science was its early use of physical instruments to study psychological function. This on-line museum provides access for students to view early research instruments such as a kymograph or a tuning fork.

Museum of the History of Psychological Instrumentation
http://www.chss.monclair.edu/psychology/museum/museum.html
This comprehensive on-line museum contains hundreds of diagrams of early psychological instruments, an explanation of their purpose, and references for further study.

On-Line Psychology Experiments
http://www.yorku.ca/dept/psych/lab/links/online.htm
This site provides access to comprehensive sites that cover on-line psychology surveys or experiments.

REFERENCES

Chernyshenko, O.S., & Ones, D.S. (1999). How selective are psychology graduate programs? The effects of selection ratio on GRE score validity.
Educational & Psychological Measurement, 59, 951-961.

Dillinger, R. & Landrum, R. E. (2002). An information course for the beginning
psychology major. Teaching of Psychology, 29(3), 230.

Edwards & Smith (1988) cited in Chapter 4 Careers

Fretz, B.R., & Strang, D.J. (1988). Preparing for Graduate Study in Psychology.
NOT for Seniors Only! Washington, DC: American Psychological
Association.

Hogan, P. M. (1991). Vocational preparation within a liberal arts framework:
Suggested directions for undergraduate psychology programs. Teaching of
Psychology, 18(3), 148-153.

House, J.D., & Johnson, J.J. (2002). Predictive validity of the Graduate Record
Examination Advanced Psychology Test for grade performance in graduate
psychology courses. College Student Journal, 36, 32-36.

James, W. (1958). Talks to Teachers, New York: W. W. Norton Co.

Kilburg, R. R. (Ed.) (1991). How to Manage Your Career in Psychology.
Washington, D.C.: APA.

Landrum, R. E. (2001). I'm getting my bachelor's degree in psychology—what can
I do with it? Eye on Psi Chi, 6(1), 22-24.

Landrum, R.E., Jeglum, E.B., & Cashin, J.R. (1994). The decision-making
processes of graduate admissions committees in psychology. Journal of
Social Behavior & Personality, 9, 239-248.

Malin, J.T., & Timmreck, C. (1979). Student goals and the undergraduate curriculum. Teaching of Psychology, 6, 136-139.

McGovern, T.V., & Hawks, B.K. (1986). The varieties of undergraduate experience. Teaching of Psychology, 13, 174-180.

McKeachie, W. J. (1999). *Teaching Tips: Strategies, Research, and Theory for College and University Teachers, 10th Ed.*. Boston, MA: Houghton, Mifflin Company.

Morgan, B. L. & Korschgen, A. (2001). Majoring in psych? Career Options for Psychology Undergraduates. (2nd Ed.). Boston: Allyn & Bacon.

Murray, B. (2002). What psych majors need to know. Monitor on Psychology, 33(7), 80-81.

Murray, B. (2002). Good news for bachelor's grads. Monitor on Psychology. 33(6), 30-32.

Murray, B. (2002). Good news for bachelor's grads. Psychology training opens doors for recent graduates. On-line. http://www.apa.org/monitor/jun02/goodnews.html

Naut, M.M. (2000). Assessing the accuracy of psychology undergraduates' perceptions of graduate admission criteria. Teaching of Psychology, 27, 277-280.

Norcross, J.C., Sayette, M.A., Mayne, T.J., Karg, R.S., & Turkson, M.A. (1988). Selecting a doctoral program in professional psychology: Some comparisons among PhD counseling, PhD clinical, and PsyD clinical psychology programs. Professional Psychology—Research & Practice, 29, 609-614.

Perlman, B. & McCann. L. I. (1999). The most frequently listed courses in the undergraduate curriculum. Teaching of Psychology, 26(3), 177-182.

Peterson's Graduate and Professional Programs, 34th Edition. (2000). Princeton, NJ: Peterson's.

Sternberg, R.J., & Williams, W.M. (1998). You proved our point better than we did: A reply to our critics. American Psychologist, 53, 576-577.

Sternberg, R.J., & Williams, W.M. (1997). Does the Graduate Record Examination predict meaningful success in the graduate training of psychologists? A case study. <u>American Psychologist, 52,</u> 630-641.

Symons, D.K. (1999). GRE predictive validity in Master's Program in Clinical Psychology. <u>Canadian Psychology, 40,</u> 71-73.

Whicker, M. L. & Kronenfeld, J. J. (1994). *Dealing with Ethical Dilemmas on Campus, Vol 14.* Thousand Oaks, CA: Sage Publications

Williams, S., Wicherski, M., & Kohout, J.L. (2000). Salaries in Psychology: 1999. [Report]. Washington DC: APA Research Office.

0-595-28954-1